By The Editors of Consumer Guide®

Plumbing Repairs Made Easy

BEEKMAN HOUSE
New York

Contents

HOW IT WORKS 4
Your home's plumbing system isn't really mysterious. Once you know the basics, you can take care of many plumbing problems yourself.
Supply and Disposal 4
Supply System 4
Drainage System 7
Putting It All Together 9

PIPES 10
Pipes are the lifelines of the plumbing system. You should know how they work and how to repair or replace them.
Types of Pipe 10
Pipe Tools 16
Working with Copper Pipe and Tubing 19
Working with Galvanized Steel Pipe 22
Working with Plastic Pipe 24
Working with Cast-Iron Pipe 25
Installing New or Replacement Pipe 27
Stopping Leaks in Pipes and Joints 28
Sweating Pipes 31
Disaster Leaks 32
Thawing Frozen Pipes 32
Quieting Noisy Pipes 34

TOILETS 37
The toilet is one of the most important fixtures. Fortunately, most toilet troubles can be remedied by any well-informed do-it-yourselfer.
Replacing a Toilet Seat 37
Specialized Tools 38

Copyright © 1980 by Publications International, Ltd.
All rights reserved
This book may not be reproduced or quoted in whole or in part by mimeograph or any other printed means or for presentation on radio or television without written permission from:
Louis Weber, President
Publications International, Ltd.
3841 West Oakton Street
Skokie, Illinois 60076
Permission is never granted for commercial purposes.

Publications International, Ltd. has made every effort to ensure accuracy and reliability of the information, instructions and directions in this book; however, it is in no way to be construed as a guarantee, and Publications International, Ltd. is not liable in case of misinterpretation of the directions, human error or typographical mistakes.

Manufactured in the United States of America
1 2 3 4 5 6 7 8 9 10

Library of Congress Catalog Card Number: 79-57308
ISBN: 0-517-301873

This edition published by:
BEEKMAN HOUSE
A Division of Crown Publishers, Inc.
One Park Avenue
New York, New York 10016

Cover Design: Frank E. Peiler
Cover Photography: Dave Jordano Photography Inc.
Illustrations: C. A. Moberg
Acknowledgment: The Editors of Consumer Guide® wish to thank Sears, Roebuck & Co. for allowing us to photograph some of their products.

Clearing a Clogged Toilet 38
Toilet Tank Troubles 39
Working with the Ballcock Assembly 41
Inadequate Flushing, Sweating, and Other Problems 43
Removing and Replacing a Toilet 44

SINKS AND TUBS 48
Every homeowner should be able to maintain and repair most sink and tub problems without having to pay for a plumber.
Tools for Sinks and Tubs 48
Eliminating Faucet Drips 49
Stopping Faucet Leaks 52
Silencing Noisy Faucets 52
Replacing a Faucet 53
Aerators 54
Repairing a Spray Head 54
Adding a Water Outlet 55
Installing a Shutoff Valve 56
Trap Replacement 57
Modernizing Lavatories and Tubs 58
Lavatory and Tub Stoppers 64
Sink Strainers 66
Tub-Shower Diverters 67
Shower Heads 67
Clearing Clogged Drains 67

PLUMBING-RELATED APPLIANCES 73
You should know how these appliances operate, how to maintain them, and how to install replacements.
Garbage Disposers 73
Clothes Washers 75
Dishwashers 78

HOT WATER SYSTEMS 84
The water heater is a very important appliance. It seldom gives trouble; but when it does, you should know what to do.
How the Water Heater Works 85
Maintenance and Repairs 88

PRIVATE SEWAGE SYSTEMS 91
Private sewage systems are similar in basic operation. At the very least, you should know how they work and how to test your septic tank.
Septic Systems 91
Testing and Cleaning the Tank 92
Disposal Fields and Seepage Pits 92
Construction and Maintenance 93

GLOSSARY 94

How It Works

Few things strike such terror in the hearts of home-owners and apartment-dwellers as the word "plumbing." Cartoonists have played upon this fear for years, picturing the hapless victim of a plumbing calamity floating on the rising waters of a flooding basement. Naturally, there is some truth in all this. Severe plumbing emergencies do arise, and there is probably no individual so lucky as never to be plagued by some type of plumbing problem.

Most likely, however, it is not really the dire events that trouble most people. Their feelings are rooted, instead, in the fear of the unknown. To them, plumbing is a mysterious system, which works in ways known only to those who belong to the union and who never seem to be available when you need them the most. Plumbing, however, works according to some basic laws of nature — gravity, pressure, water seeking its own level — that you can understand in no time. There is little mystery about how your plumbing system works, but there often is a great deal of misunderstanding. Once you know the basics, you can take care of a great many plumbing problems yourself — and save yourself time, trouble, and money in the process.

SUPPLY AND DISPOSAL

The plumbing in your home is one system composed of two complementary but entirely separate subsystems. One subsystem brings fresh water in, and the other subsystem takes waste water out. Naturally, if you and your family are to stay healthy, you must avoid any cross-connection between the supply and disposal subsystems.

If you live in an urban or suburban area, your fresh water is probably pumped to you by the community water department, and your waste water is carried off via a main sewer line to a collective sewage-treatment facility. If you live in a fairly remote or rural area, however, there is a good chance that you depend on a private well for your water supply and a septic tank for waste disposal. As you might expect, the collective systems for supply and drainage are more efficient than the private systems. That is not to say that the private facilities do not work well; rather, it means that more people can be served at less cost when they are linked to a central community water department and sewage-treatment plant.

SUPPLY SYSTEM

Water that comes into your home does so under pressure. It makes no difference whether your water supply is public or private; water that comes from either a storage tank or a well enters your home under enough pressure to allow it to travel upstairs, around corners or wherever else it is needed.

In urban and suburban areas, the community water department pumps water into a tank or tower that is higher than the surrounding homes; the force of gravity supplies the water pressure. If you have your own well, you probably have a pump to bring water into your home under pressure. Occasionally, homes linked to a central municipal supply suffer from insufficient water pressure, and these homes must then add a pump similar to those used for private wells.

Water leaves the tank or tower and travels through a water main to the supply line for your home. Before you actually use the water for drinking, bathing, washing clothes and dishes, and so on, it may pass through a meter that registers the number of gallons or cubic feet you consume. The water meter may be somewhere on your property outside the house, or it may be inside at the point where the supply pipe enters. The outside type of meter has a metal cover over it; you can lift the cover for access to the meter.

Even if you never care to look at the water meter itself, you should be familiar with one device that is generally located close to the meter. That is the main shutoff or stop valve. In a plumbing emergency, it is vital that you be able to get to and close the main shutoff valve as fast as you possibly can. When a pipe bursts, for example, it can flood your house in no time; but you can minimize damage by closing the main shutoff valve to shut off all the water coming into the house. The shutoff may be a stop-and-waste valve that drains the water from the pipes as well as shuts off the supply. Naturally, if the emergency is confined to a sink, tub or toilet, you may not want to cut the house's entire water supply. Therefore, most fixtures have — or should have — individual supply stop valves.

Once the water has passed from the public facility's tower or tank through the main supply line to your individual supply line and through your home water meter and main shutoff valve, it travels to the different fixtures in the house for your use. It is ready, that is, for all your

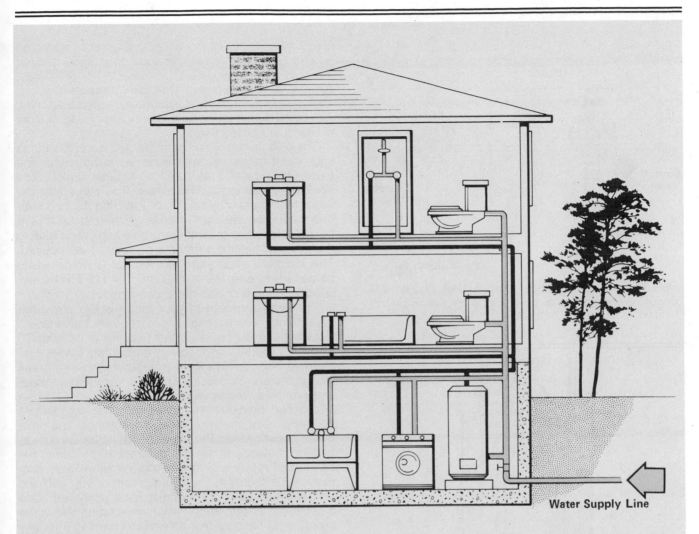

Water enters your home under pressure to allow it to travel upstairs, around corners or wherever else it is needed.

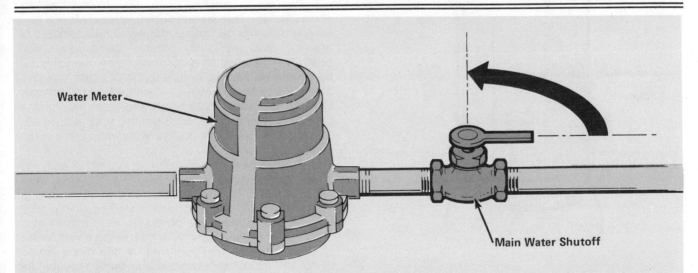

Water Meter

Main Water Shutoff

As water comes into your home, it passes through a meter that registers the amount you use. Generally the main water shutoff or stop valve is located close to the meter.

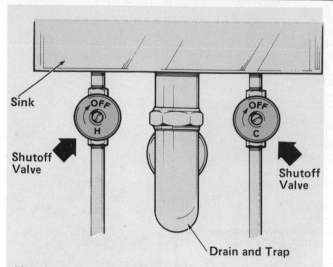

Sink

Shutoff Valve

Shutoff Valve

Drain and Trap

Most fixtures have—or should have—individual supply shutoff valves so that you need not close the main shutoff to make repairs at the fixture.

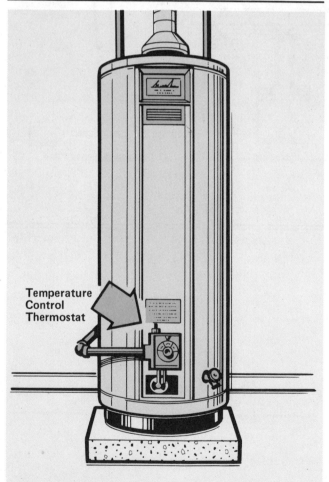

Temperature Control Thermostat

A thermostat on your water heater maintains the temperature you select by turning the heating device on and off as required.

cold water needs. All the water that enters your home is, of course, cold water. As such, it is piped through the cold water distribution lines directly to all fixtures, outlets, and appliances that use unheated water; offshoots to the individual fixtures are called branches. The pipes that run vertically, extending upward a story or more, are called risers.

One pipe carries water from the cold water system to your water heater. From the heater, a hot water line carries the heated water to all the fixtures, outlets, and appliances that require hot water. You can adjust the water temperature by raising or lowering the temperature setting on the water heater. A thermostat on the heater maintains the temperature you select by turning the device's heating elements on and off as required. The normal temperature setting for a home water heater is between 140° and 160°F, but 120°F is usually adequate and it is also more economical.

The water pressure in your home is like any other good thing; too much of it can be very bad indeed. Residential water pressure that reaches or exceeds 70 to 80 psi (pounds per square inch) can cause your pipes to bang and faucets to leak. It also can break pipe joints and connections. At the very least, excessive pressure wastes water.

You can measure the average water pressure in your house by attaching a pressure gauge to a cold-water faucet nearest the main shutoff valve. Be sure to test the pressure at several different times during the day to find a true average. Water pressure does fluctuate, but it should not fluctuate greatly or you will have an uncomfortable time trying to take a shower. One other thing to remember when measuring the water pressure: Make sure that no water is running from any other outlet in your home besides the one to which the gauge is attached.

If the gauge registers 70 to 80 psi or more, you should install a pressure-reducing valve. This is a fairly inexpensive device, and a do-it-yourselfer should be able to install one easily. Most of these valves work best when installed on a horizontal pipe; the valve can be connected into the supply line with union fittings — fittings used to join pipes — without much difficulty. Once it is installed, you can merely set the valve to provide the water pressure that best suits your needs. The valve will lower the pressure and maintain it at that setting.

Decreasing excessive water pressure is easy; increasing inadequate water pressure is, however, much more difficult. You can reduce the 70-to-80 psi flow for the relatively small cost of a pressure-reducing valve, but trying to increase the pressure could require such major projects as building your own water tower, installing a pump, or even ripping out all the pipes in your home and installing new ones. For those reasons, too little water pressure is something many people learn to accept and live with.

DRAINAGE SYSTEM

Just as the fresh water supply can come from either public or private facilities, the waste water drainage can go to either a public sewer line or private septic tank. Like the public supply facilities, collective sewer systems are much more convenient than private waste disposal methods. After the waste drains from individual houses into a network of pipes, it is carried to a sewage-treatment plant where it is aerated to hasten bacteriological breakdown. Solids are settled out and used for fertilizer, while the liquid is chlorinated and discharged into natural water supplies like streams, rivers, and lakes.

A septic tank and disposal field are designed to handle the waste of a single home. The tank, like the public facility, separates solids from liquid. The solids settle to the bottom of the tank, while the liquid runs out through a network of pipes into the disposal field. The tank, of course, must be cleaned every few years, and the disposal field — composed of pipes in underground trenches or pits — must be enlarged as it becomes clogged with waste matter that did not settle out completely in the tank.

No matter which method of ultimate waste disposal is used, the drainage systems in homes are essentially the same. Drainage systems do not depend on pressure as do supply systems. Instead, the waste matter leaves your house because the drainage pipes all pitch or angle downward; gravity pulls the waste along. The sewer line continues this downward flow to the sewage-treatment facility or to the septic tank.

While the system sounds simple — and it is — there is more to waste drainage than pipes tilted downward. There are also vents, traps, and clean-outs. You can see the vents sticking out of the roof of your house. They allow air to enter the drainpipes. If there was no air supply coming from the vents, waste water would not flow out properly and the water in the traps could be siphoned away.

Traps, of course, are vital components of the drainage system. You can see a trap under every sink or lavatory; it is the curved or S-shaped section of pipe under a sink's drain. Water flows from the basin with enough force to go through the trap and on out through the drainpipe, but enough water stays in the trap to form a seal that prevents sewer gas backing up into your home. If there were no seal there, bad odors and dangerous gases could enter your home.

Every fixture must have a trap. Toilets are self-trapped; they do not require an additional trap at the drain. Bathtubs frequently have drum traps; these not only form a seal against sewer gas, but also collect hair and dirt to prevent clogged drains. Grease traps in some kitchens are similar in that they collect grease that goes down the sink drain which might otherwise cause clogging. Because grease and hair are generally

Water pressure can be measured by attaching a pressure gauge to a cold water faucet nearest the main shutoff.

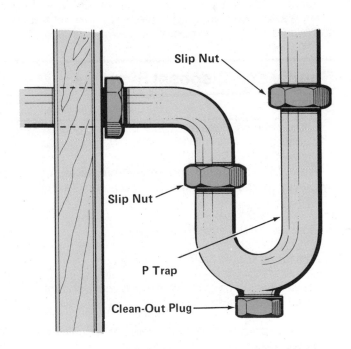

Slip Nut

Slip Nut

P Trap

Clean-Out Plug

Every fixture must have a trap to prevent sewer gas from backing up into your home.

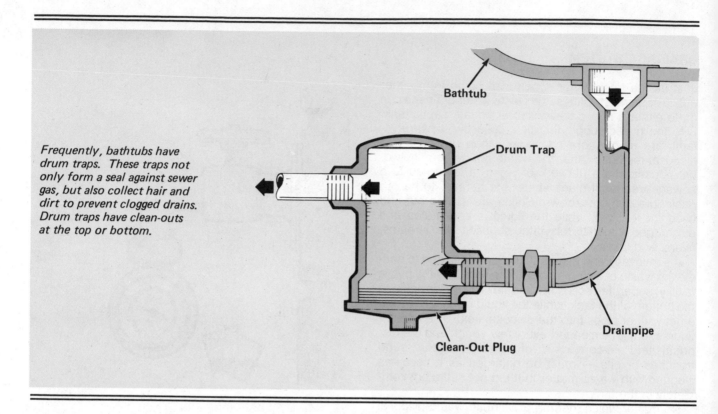

Frequently, bathtubs have drum traps. These traps not only form a seal against sewer gas, but also collect hair and dirt to prevent clogged drains. Drum traps have clean-outs at the top or bottom.

Bathtub

Drum Trap

Clean-Out Plug

Drainpipe

the causes of drain clogs, these traps have clean-out plugs that give you easier access to remove or break up any clogs.

Since the drainage system involves all of these components, it is usually referred to as the DWV — the drain, waste, vent system. If water is to flow out freely and waste is to exit properly, all components of the

DWV must be present and in good working order. Examine the pipes in your basement or crawl space. The larger and heavier pipes are for drainage. It is always a good idea to tag as many pipes as possible to know exactly what each one does. In addition, try to locate the clean-out plugs on the traps and in the drainage lines, and make sure you know where all the vents are.

Supply and Disposal Systems

SUPPLY

1. Source can be municipal water company or a private well.

2. Water flow results from pressure—created either by gravity (tall tank) or by mechanical means (water pump).

3. Flow can be up, down or sideways.

4. All fixtures should have shutoff valves.

5. Supply system must operate *totally* independent of the disposal system.

6. Possible defects: leaks, drips, noises, insufficient pressure, excessive pressure, freezing, condensation, flow restrictions from scale and water chemicals.

DISPOSAL

1. Destination can be municipal sewage-treatment plant or private septic tank.

2. Waste flow results from gravitational pull.

3. Flow is always downward.

4. All fixtures must have traps.

5. Disposal system must operate *totally* independent of the supply system.

6. Possible defects: clogs, noises, freezing, improper venting.

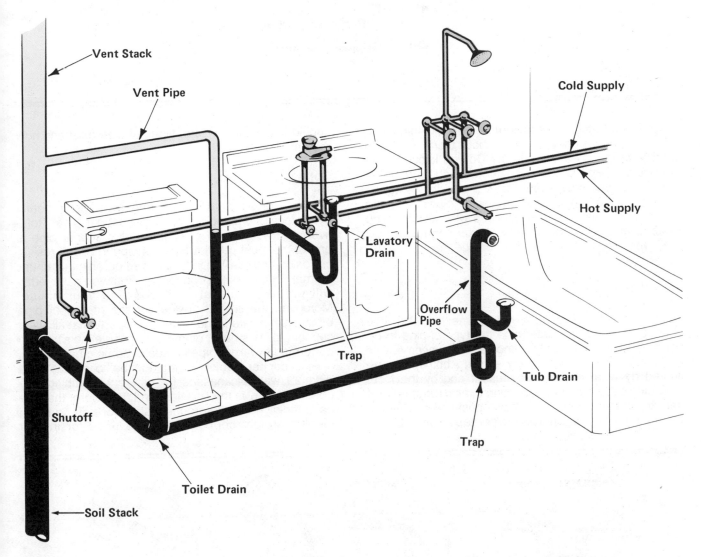

Vent Stack

Vent Pipe

Cold Supply

Hot Supply

Lavatory Drain

Overflow Pipe

Trap

Tub Drain

Shutoff

Trap

Toilet Drain

Soil Stack

Your home's supply and drainage systems must always be two distinct subsystems with no overlapping whatsoever.

PUTTING IT ALL TOGETHER

The supply and drainage subsystems are — and must always be — two distinct operations with no overlapping whatsoever. There is a "bridge" between the two, however, and the bridge is what makes the plumbing system worth having. Plumbing jargon refers to any bridge between the supply and drainage systems as a fixture.

Toilets, sinks, tubs — these are all fixtures; but there are plenty more. An outside hydrant is a fixture and so is an automatic washing machine. All devices that draw fresh water and discharge waste water are fixtures,

and all are designed to keep the supply and drainage systems they depend upon strictly segregated.

Supply, fixtures, drainage — that is all there is to plumbing. Is that anything to fear? Of course not! The fact that the system is usually hidden in the walls, under the floors, and beneath the ground may make plumbing seem mysterious, but it is really a simple and logical system. Get to know how your plumbing works and you never need fear becoming one of those hapless victims that cartoonists love to portray. In fact, once you understand plumbing, you should be able to save yourself plenty of money the next time a plumbing problem presents itself in your home or apartment.

Pipes

Take a look at the pipes in your home's plumbing system. How much do you know about them? Can you identify what they are made of? Do you know how to remove a broken section of pipe and install a replacement? Can you stop a leak, thaw a pipe that is frozen solid, or eliminate the noise caused by pipes that bang constantly? Pipes are the lifelines of your plumbing system, and you should know all you can about how they work and how to repair or replace them when, for some reason, they fail.

TYPES OF PIPE

Unless you are building a new home, there is little chance that you can determine the type of pipe to be used in your house. Your choice of replacement or additional pipe in an already existing home may be limited by what is there at present and by the local plumbing code. The code, of course, also dictates what can and cannot be used in new construction. Despite the fact that your choice is, perhaps, limited, you

should at least know what types of pipe exist and how they are used.

Copper Pipe

One type of pipe that is on the approved list in nearly every local plumbing code is rigid copper pipe. Relatively lightweight and easy to handle, copper pipe is one of the most popular types of pipe in use. It resists corrosion and scaling; in fact, it is so durable that under normal conditions the copper pipe that you have today will probably outlast both you and your house. Moreover, the smooth inside surface of copper pipe offers little resistance to water, a property that allows a copper pipe of smaller diameter to handle the same job performed by larger pipes made of some other metals.

Rigid copper pipe or "plumbing tube" comes in three different wall thicknesses for different plumbing purposes. Type K is the heaviest and, therefore, the type used mainly for underground installations. Type L is a medium-weight copper pipe; it is used for interior

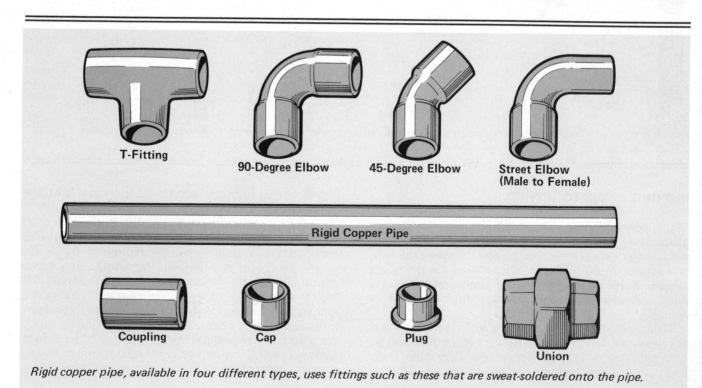

T-Fitting   90-Degree Elbow   45-Degree Elbow   Street Elbow (Male to Female)

Rigid Copper Pipe

Coupling   Cap   Plug   Union

Rigid copper pipe, available in four different types, uses fittings such as these that are sweat-soldered onto the pipe.

plumbing. Type M is the lightest copper pipe, and it is also used — where local plumbing codes permit — for interior plumbing. Even though some local codes do not allow the use of Type M copper pipe, it is adequate for most above-ground home plumbing requirements. Nevertheless, if your local plumbing code prohibits Type M, use some other weight of copper or another kind of pipe.

There is one more kind of rigid copper pipe. It is called DWV, and it is used only for drain, waste, and vent applications. DWV is even thinner-walled than Type M copper pipe, and some plumbing codes forbid it just as they do Type M. Unlike Type M, however, DWV copper pipe does not have to withstand any pressure. In a supply system, wall thickness is very important, but it is not as crucial a consideration in the drainage system. Nevertheless, if the local plumbing code says no to copper DWV, select another type of pipe.

Flexible Copper Tubing

You can buy flexible copper tubing only in Type K (designed for hard use) and Type L (for most other applications), but that disadvantage is about the only one you will encounter. Flexible copper tubing can do just about anything that rigid copper pipe can do, and plenty more besides. You can bend the tubing around corners or snake it through walls and over ceilings more easily than you can maneuver rigid copper pipe. However, installations made with flexible copper tubing are not as neat as those made with rigid copper pipe. So, flexible tubing usually is used where it will be concealed from view. Its biggest advantage, though, is in the fact that it comes in rolls of up to 100 feet or more. When you work with rigid copper pipe, you usually must sweat-solder sections to be joined, and every connection is a potential source for a leak. With flexible copper tubing, however, you just unroll the length you need; the only connections you have to make are at each end of the run. Fewer joints, of course, mean fewer chances for a leak and allow a better water flow.

Keep in mind that the larger the diameter of the tubing, the easier it is to get a kink — which is the last thing you want to have happen to copper tubing. The tube need not stay perfectly round, but a kink will restrict water flow and form a weak spot in the pipe. You can form gradual bends in flexible copper tubing just by using your hands. If you need to make a sharp turn, however, do not try to do it by hand; use a tube bender, a spring-like tool that is designed specifically for this purpose.

Galvanized Steel Pipe

Although copper pipe and tubing have replaced galvanized steel pipe as the most popular type for new home water supply lines, galvanized pipe — which used to hold a monopoly on the supply pipe market — still offers some distinct advantages. For example, suppose your pipes run through a garage or basement or any other area where they are exposed to blows

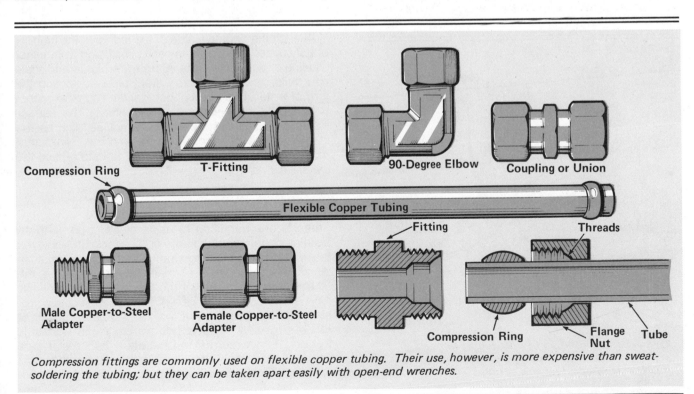

Compression Ring   T-Fitting   90-Degree Elbow   Coupling or Union

Flexible Copper Tubing

Fitting   Threads

Male Copper-to-Steel Adapter   Female Copper-to-Steel Adapter   Compression Ring   Flange Nut   Tube

Compression fittings are commonly used on flexible copper tubing. Their use, however, is more expensive than sweat-soldering the tubing; but they can be taken apart easily with open-end wrenches.

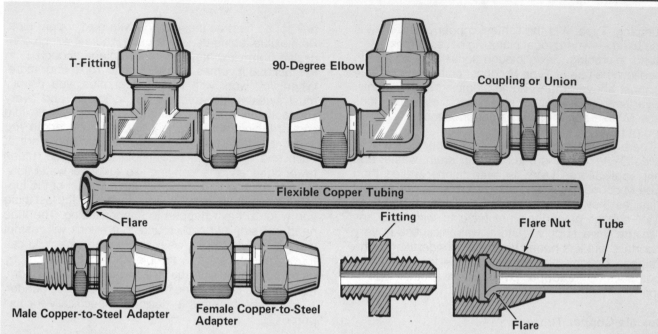

T-Fitting

90-Degree Elbow

Coupling or Union

Flexible Copper Tubing

Flare

Fitting

Flare Nut

Tube

Male Copper-to-Steel Adapter

Female Copper-to-Steel Adapter

Flare

Flare fittings, also used on flexible copper tubing, offer the same advantages and disadvantages as compression fittings. However, they require a special tool to flare the end of the tubing.

from cars or tools. For such situations, you would be much smarter to use galvanized steel pipe because it is very tough and much better able to withstand damaging shocks.

The price you pay for using galvanized steel pipe is both an advantage and a disadvantage. On one hand,

galvanized pipe is much less expensive than copper at the time of initial purchase. On the other hand, galvanized pipe is much more expensive to repair. It takes so much longer to cut, thread, and join galvanized pipe than it does for copper pipe or tubing that labor costs will be very high if you have to call in a professional plumber.

Also on the negative side of the ledger is the inability of galvanized steel pipe to resist corrosion from either alkaline or acidic deposits in the water. Lime and scale can build up in galvanized steel pipe, restricting the flow of water. Even at its best, galvanized pipe cannot match copper for water-flow properties. The surface inside a galvanized steel pipe is not as slick as the inside surface of a copper pipe, and the fittings that must be used with galvanized pipe tend to reduce the water-flow as well.

Plastic Pipe

There is one handicap to using plastic pipe — many building codes prohibit some or all uses of it. However, these codes are likely to change in the future because plastic pipe possesses so many fine features. It is difficult to say which one of the many aspects of plastic pipe is its most advantageous. It is not subject to corrosion, scaling or rust; it is virtually self-cleaning; it will not rot, and usually it does not sweat; it can withstand freezing temperatures much better than metal pipe can; and it is so light that plastic pipe is easier to handle than just about any other kind of pipe. In addition, be-

Tubing

Tube Bender

To make sharp bends in flexible tubing without kinking it, you can use a tube-bender, a spring-like tool that is designed for this purpose.

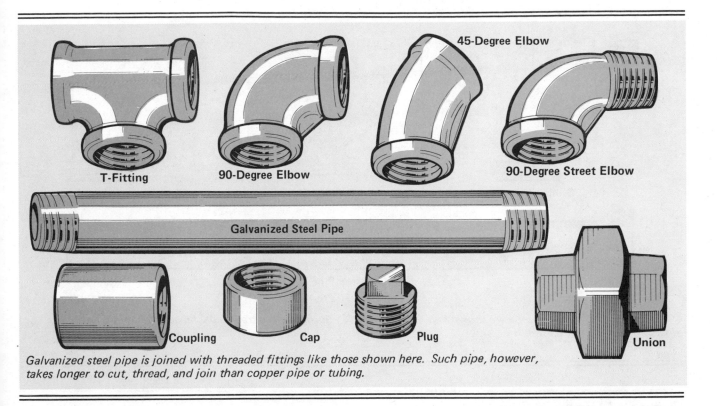

45-Degree Elbow

T-Fitting

90-Degree Elbow

90-Degree Street Elbow

Galvanized Steel Pipe

Coupling

Cap

Plug

Union

Galvanized steel pipe is joined with threaded fittings like those shown here. Such pipe, however, takes longer to cut, thread, and join than copper pipe or tubing.

cause plastic is a more flexible substance than metal, plastic supply lines virtually eliminate water hammer and the need for installing air chambers; it damps vibrations and does not carry sound well. Plastic pipe has low resistance to water flow and consequent excellent flow rates; it is the easiest of all piping to install,

especially for the do-it-yourselfer. Finally, plastic pipe is less expensive than even galvanized steel pipe.

There are several types of plastic pipe in common use today for various home plumbing applications. CPVC (chlorinated polyvinyl chloride) pipe is rigid and used for hot and cold water distribution systems. PB

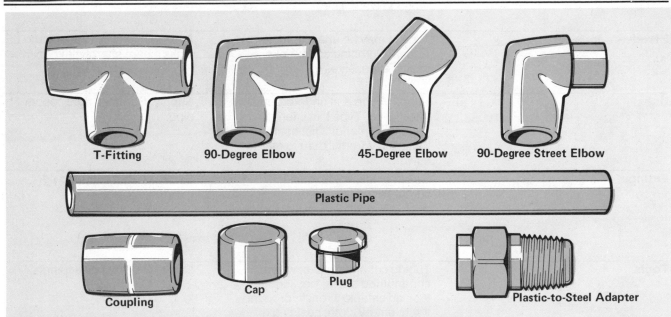

T-Fitting

90-Degree Elbow

45-Degree Elbow

90-Degree Street Elbow

Plastic Pipe

Coupling

Cap

Plug

Plastic-to-Steel Adapter

Although some types of plastic pipe are joined with threaded and other kinds of fittings, much of it is connected with fittings that are solvent-welded to the pipe, such as the ones shown above.

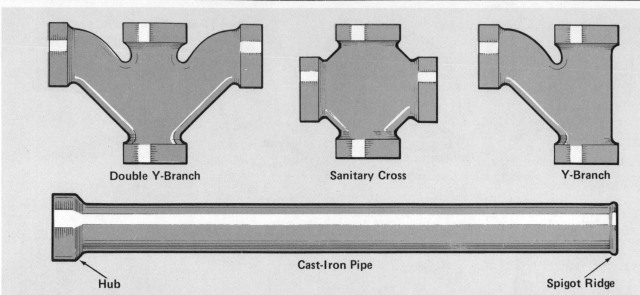

Double Y-Branch   Sanitary Cross   Y-Branch

Cast-Iron Pipe

Hub   Spigot Ridge

Some fittings for cast-iron pipe are shown here and on page 15. Such pipe is a traditional favorite when it comes to installing soil and waste drains.

Types of Pipe

	RIGID COPPER	COPPER TUBING
Varieties	Types K, L, M, and DWV.	Types K, L.
Characteristics	Resists corrosion and scaling; light, durable, easy to handle; has smooth interior surface for good water flow.	All advantages of rigid copper pipe plus easy bending.
Disadvantages	Type M may be unacceptable to local plumbing code; kinks easily; expensive.	Available only in Types K and L; kinks if bent sharply; expensive.
Uses	Supply: Type K in underground installation, Type L in interior, Type M in interior. Disposal: Type DWV from fixture to main sewer.	Supply: Same as rigid copper pipe.
Fittings	Sweat-soldered; flare and compression fittings.	Same as rigid copper pipe.
Tools	Tubing cutter or hacksaw with fine-toothed blade; file; flaring tool; adjustable wrench; propane torch; emery cloth; paste flux; solder.	Same as rigid copper pipe.

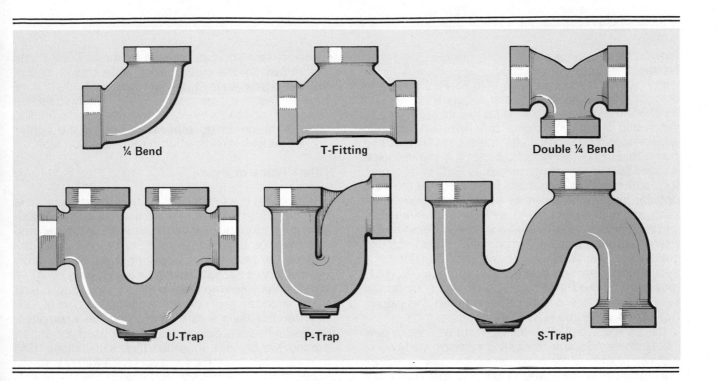

¼ Bend   T-Fitting   Double ¼ Bend

U-Trap   P-Trap   S-Trap

Types of Pipe

GALVANIZED STEEL	PLASTIC	CAST IRON
One type.	ABS, CPVC, PB, PE, PP, PVC, SR.	Service, extra-heavy.
Resists shocks and impact blows; less expensive than copper to install initially.	Does not rust or corrode; self-cleaning; lightweight; usually does not sweat or freeze; excellent water flow; inexpensive.	Durable; corrosion-free.
Difficult and expensive to repair; corrodes from acid or alkaline; subject to lime and scale deposits; inferior water flow.	Unacceptable to many local plumbing codes; many types cannot handle hot water supply.	Cutting and joining difficult and time-consuming; heavy to work with.
Supply: In areas where pipes are subject to damage.	Various types suitable for drain, waste, vent systems; irrigation systems; building sewers, sewer mains; hot and cold water distribution.	Disposal: Especially used in underground installations.
Threaded joints.	Various types connected by solvent-welding, transition fittings, threading, flanging, insert fittings, flare fittings, butt and socket fusion, mechanical couplings, compression fittings.	Bell-and-spigot, gasket, and no-hub connections.
Pipe cutter or hacksaw and vise; pipe die cutter; cutting oil; file; pipe reamer; pipe joint compound; pipe wrenches.	Fine-toothed hacksaw or plastic-pipe cutter; miter box; cleaner; solvent cement; brush; file; utility knife.	Hacksaw; cold chisel; heavy hammer; oakum; yarning iron; lead; lead pot and ladle; caulking tool; joint runner; screwdriver.

(polybutylene) pipe is a new, highly flexible tubing used for the same purpose as CPVC pipe, as well as for water supply lines. One form of rigid PVC (polyvinyl chloride) pipe is made for water supply lines, another for DWV systems, and a third for sewer lines and underground drainage systems. It is also used for cold water distribution and drainage traps and their assorted parts. Rigid ABS (acrylonitrile-butadiene styrene) pipe is made for the same applications as PVC pipe, except for water supply or distribution uses. Perhaps the most popular plastic pipe for water supply lines, lawn sprinkling, and irrigation purposes is PE (polyethylene) pipe, which is flexible and available in several grades. SR (styrene rubber) pipe is used primarily for underground drainage systems, while PP (polypropylene) pipe is available in plumbing fixture traps, tailpieces, trap extensions and their associated parts, and is by far the best choice for new or replacement gear of this nature. Both SR and PP are rigid types of pipe.

All of these types of plastic pipe can be used in new installations, additions to existing systems made up of metallic piping, or for repair work, because adapters are available to allow you to connect just about any type of pipe to just about any other type. However, check your local plumbing code carefully and if the code does not prohibit plastic pipe, or if it does and you can obtain a variance, give plastic pipe serious consideration for your next plumbing installation or repair.

Cast-Iron Pipe

When it comes to soil and waste pipes, the traditional favorite is cast iron. It is so very durable and practically corrosion-free that it can be used for underground installations with no problems. In most home drainage systems, cast-iron pipe is used for the soil and waste stacks (and for the main drains), while copper tube of the DWV type is used for the branches to the fixture drains. Cast-iron pipe comes in two weights: service (standard) and extra heavy. Unless your local plumbing code tells you to do otherwise, opt for the lighter service-weight version when buying cast-iron pipe.

Other Types of Pipe

When weight is a factor and underground installation is not, steel drain pipes are often used in place of cast-iron ones. Much lighter than cast-iron pipe, steel pipe can never be used underground because it could collapse under the weight of the earth. Lead pipe is rarely used anymore except sometimes as a "closet bend" — the pipe that joins the toilet to the soil pipe. Septic tank systems occasionally employ a perforated type of fiber pipe for releasing waste liquids into the drain field. Asbestos-cement pipe is sometimes used for underground sewer lines in septic tank installations, and brass is common in traps and was once widely installed in home water distribution systems.

PIPE TOOLS

If you plan to do a fair amount of plumbing repairs yourself, your tools become very important. Many plumbing tools, of course, can be used for other do-it-yourself tasks around the house; but no matter how much or how little you plan to use a particular tool, it should be the best of its type that you can afford. Often a good tool will last a lifetime, whereas a poor tool may not make it through the project for which you bought it.

Although the tools you decide to purchase depend

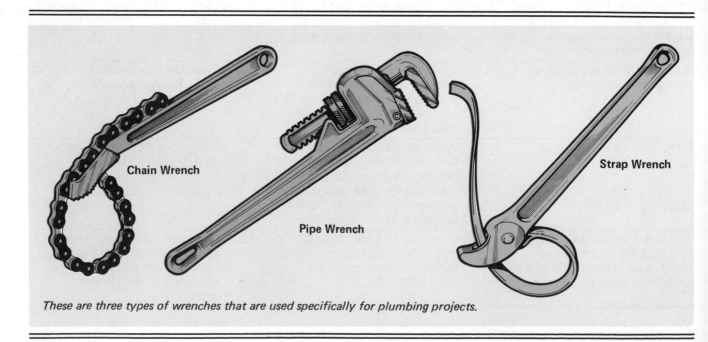

Chain Wrench

Pipe Wrench

Strap Wrench

These are three types of wrenches that are used specifically for plumbing projects.

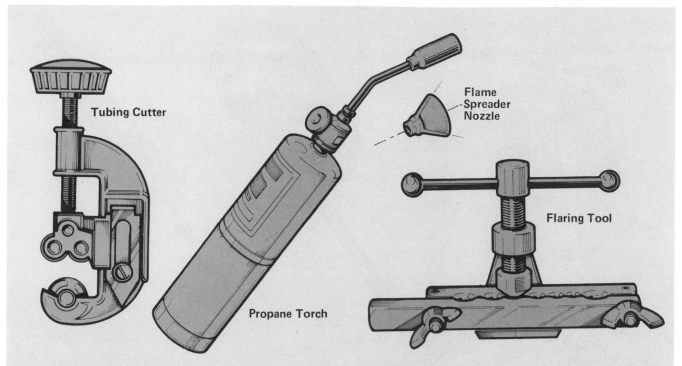

Working with copper pipe or tubing can require some special tools, such as a tubing cutter, propane torch and a flaring tool.

on how deeply you are involved in home repairs in general and in plumbing projects in particular, there are certain basic tools that any self-respecting do-it-yourself plumber should have in his toolbox. For working with galvanized steel or cast-iron pipes, you will need pipe wrenches. These wrenches are generally used in pairs; one holds like a vise while the other turns a fitting or a pipe. A chain wrench is designed for larger galvanized steel or cast-iron pipes, and a strap wrench — which works on the same principle as the chain wrench — can be used on polished or plastic pipe without damaging them.

Copper pipe and copper tubing require some special tools. Since you should avoid using a hacksaw on copper pipe, be sure to have a tubing cutter in your toolbox. A small-size cutter, moreover, makes it much easier to work in close quarters, and you will be amazed at how many plumbing chores are performed in cramped surroundings. You will also need a propane torch for sweat-soldering and a flaring tool for making flare connections at pipe joints.

Just like copper pipes, galvanized steel pipes also require some special tools. When cutting such pipe, you should have a combination vise — one that has a section with pipe jaws — or a yoke or a chain vise, both of which are made especially for pipe work. A pipe cutter tool is easier to use than a hacksaw, but be sure that the cutter is designed for galvanized steel pipes;

the tubing cutter for copper is very similar in appearance. Of course, you must be prepared to remove the burrs created by cutting. Outside burrs can be removed with a file, but you will need a reamer to remove any burrs inside the pipe.

Although you can generally purchase the galvanized steel pipe you need already threaded, you may wish to do your own threading. If so, you will need special dies that come in sizes for threading all standard pipe diameters. Whenever you are cutting or threading pipe you should use a cutting oil. And, speaking of oil, a can of penetrating oil can come in handy when you tackle a plumbing repair job.

Very few tools — none of them special — are needed for working with plastic pipe. Rigid plastic pipe can be cut with a fine-toothed hacksaw (or, if you prefer, a plastic-tubing cutter); flexible types can be cut with a sharp knife. On most common types of plastic pipe, fittings are joined with solvent cement. On other types, usually compression or threaded fittings are used; they are simply tightened with an adjustable open-end wrench.

For sealing large cast-iron drainpipes against leaks, you will need a caulking tool for packing the oakum into the joint, a melting pot for heating the lead, and a ladle for pouring the molten lead over the oakum. When you work on horizontal drainpipes, moreover, you face the problem of keeping the molten lead in the joint and

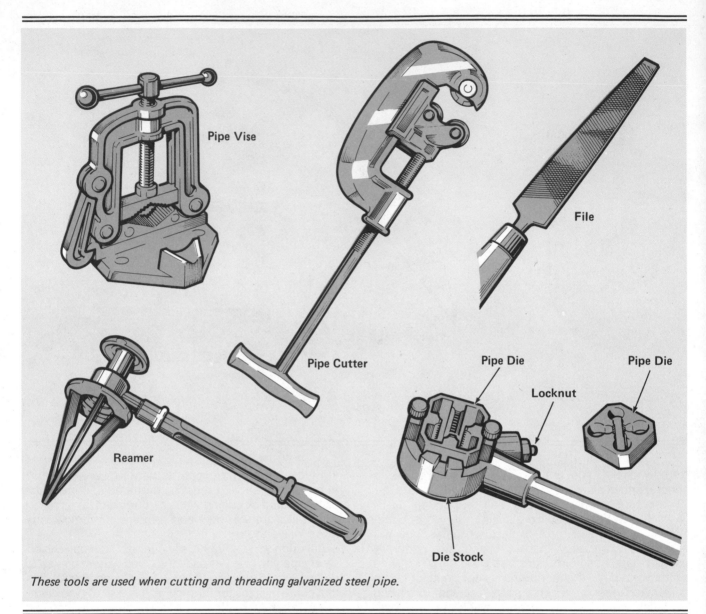

Pipe Vise

Pipe Cutter

File

Reamer

Pipe Die

Locknut

Pipe Die

Die Stock

These tools are used when cutting and threading galvanized steel pipe.

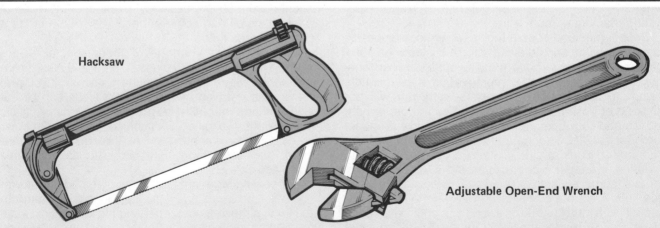

Hacksaw

Adjustable Open-End Wrench

Cutting and joining plastic pipe requires few tools. Two that may be useful are a fine-toothed hacksaw for cutting rigid pipe and an adjustable wrench for plastic pipe with certain types of fittings.

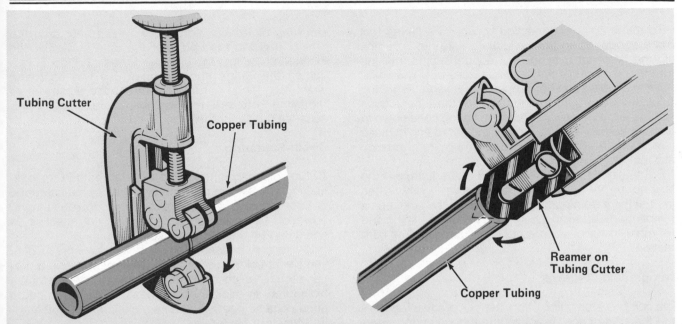

To avoid damaging the ends of copper pipe, a tubing cutter should be used (left). Any burrs inside the cut end of the pipe must be removed (right); the outside can be cleaned with sandpaper or emery cloth.

preventing it from running out on the ground. The answer to this problem is a special tool called an asbestos joint runner.

WORKING WITH COPPER PIPE AND TUBING

Cutting copper pipe or tubing without kinking it takes care. So avoid sawing copper, if possible; use a tubing cutter instead. Of course, a tubing cutter will be of little use on the larger-sized copper pipes. For those you must use a hacksaw, but be sure to equip it with the finest-toothed blade you can find. Saw as straight as possible — using a miter box will help to obtain a square cut. Eliminate any irregularities in the edge — as well as any burrs both inside and out — with a file. If you must put the copper pipe in a vise to hold it while you saw, clamp the vise on the pipe as far away from where you are cutting as possible so that you do not dent the end of the tubing or pipe. Anything but a perfectly round end will not connect well to another section of pipe or tube.

Copper pipes or tubes can be joined in several ways. Sweat-soldering is the most common and least expensive way of joining copper pipe, while flare fittings and compression fittings are used mainly for flexible tubing.

Flared Fittings

The advantages to a flare fitting are that it can be taken apart easily with a pair of open-end wrenches; and it can be used in situations where sweat-soldering is either dangerous (fire hazard) or impossible (uncon-

trollably wet conditions). The disadvantage is that flare fittings are much more expensive than the ones you sweat-solder.

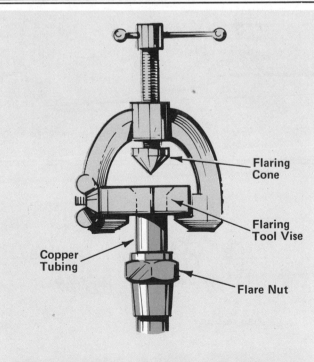

To flare the end of copper tubing, slip the flare nut over the end of the tubing, insert the tubing into the flaring tool vise, and turn down the flaring cone.

To make a flare connection you need a flaring tool and a special fitting that includes a flare nut. You first slip the flare nut over the cut copper tubing, making sure that the open end of the nut faces out. Then, you insert the tubing into the proper-size hole in the flaring tool vise. Make sure the cut edge of the tube is flush with the edge of the vise. Turn the flaring cone down to flare the end of the tube. Inspect the flared end to make sure that it is even, that there are no burrs or cracks, and that the tube surface is completely clean.

Put the fitting into the flared end of the tube, pull the flare nut up to it, and turn the nut down tightly. When you get the flare nut as tight as you can by hand, use a pair of open-end wrenches — one to hold the fitting and the other to turn the flare nut — to complete the connection.

Compression Fittings

The compression fitting offers the same advantages — and the same price disadvantage in relation to sweat-soldering — as does the flare fitting, but it does not require a flaring tool. Actually, compression fittings are much like flare fittings, but without the flare. A compression fitting has the same two parts as the flare fitting, but the compression fitting also has a compres-

sion ring or ferrule. You slip the flange nut onto the tubing, and slip the ring over the tube as well. Then insert the tube into the fitting as far as it will go. Hand-tighten the flange nut, and then use two open-end wrenches — one to turn the nut and the other to hold the fitting — to seal the ring against the fitting and to squeeze it against the tube.

Sweat-Soldering

Sweat-soldering is the most popular method for connecting copper pipes. Done properly, sweat-soldering is both effective and inexpensive. If not done right, however, sweat-soldering certainly is not effective — and it can be disastrously expensive.

Unlike conventional soldering with an iron or gun, you sweat-solder with a torch. Most people use a propane torch, which is easier and safer to operate than a blow-torch. In addition to the heat source, you need a good nonacid paste flux, emery cloth, and 50/50 lead-tin solid-core solder.

At least as important as having the right materials is properly preparing the pipe to be sweat-soldered. There are three key factors necessary to assure good sweat-soldered joints: clean copper, totally dry pipes, and proper heat. If you are dealing with newly cut pipe

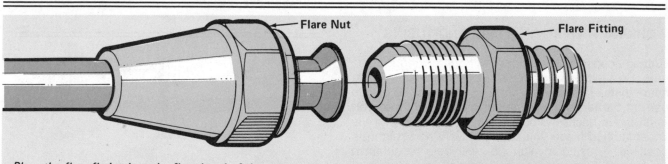

Place the flare fitting into the flared end of the tube, pull the nut up to it, and turn the nut down tightly.

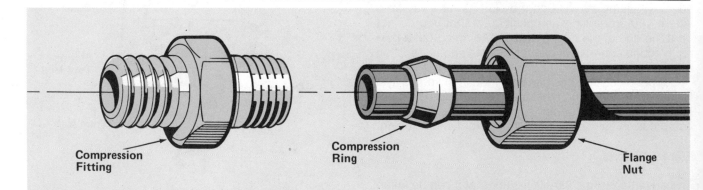

Compression fittings are much like flare fittings, but without the flare. The flange nut and compression ring are slipped onto the tubing, which is then inserted into the fitting. The flange nut is tightened to secure the joint.

or tubing, be sure to remove all burrs from both the inside and outside of the cut end. Of course, if the cut end of the tube has been bent or crushed in the cutting process, start over with a freshly cut length of pipe; the end should be perfectly round. Then, check the fittings to be sure that the joint will be tight.

Caution: One of the most crucial factors in sweat-soldering is making sure that all the pipes and fittings are completely dry. If there is any residual moisture, it will turn to steam when the pipes are heated, and the end result will be a weak or even a leaking joint. The build-up of trapped steam in a pipe could also cause an explosion. Therefore, before you actually start putting the pieces together, make absolutely certain that no moisture is lurking anywhere. If you are soldering on part of your plumbing system, drain the pipes and leave the faucets open so steam buildup can escape.

There are a couple of techniques that will help you to dry the pipes thoroughly. If you are sweat-soldering to a vertical pipe, you can use a rag to remove any moisture; but if the connection is to be made to part of a horizontal run of pipe, try this plumbing trick. Wad a piece of white bread into a ball, poke the bread ball into the pipe, and push it back beyond the area you will be soldering. The bread will absorb moisture that might otherwise reach the joint and ruin your sweat-soldering. When the job is done and you turn the water back on, the bread will dissolve; the residue will come out through the nearest open tap.

Now, clean all the metal surfaces that you plan to join. Fine steel wool or fine sandpaper can be used for the job. However, the best way to clean the outside of a pipe is to wrap an emery cloth strip around the tubing or pipe and go back and forth as if you were buffing a shoe. You want the metal to shine, but be careful not to overdo it. The last thing you want to do is to take away so much metal that you lose the snug fit. On the other hand, do not forget to clean every surface that will be part of the sweat-soldered joint, including inside the fitting where the pipe will go.

When you have cleaned the pipe and fitting, coat all the cleaned metal surfaces with a paste flux that is especially compounded for soldering copper. Spread the flux on both the pipe and the fitting with your fingers, an old toothbrush, or a small, stiff paintbrush. Insert the pipe into the fitting and rotate them a bit to distribute the paste evenly around the joint.

Once you have applied the flux and joined the pipe to the fitting, you are ready to solder. Light your propane torch and get the solid-core solder ready in your other hand. You will have to heat the copper to about 400°F. Play the flame over the fitting — not the pipe. Do not put the flame on the solder; the solder should melt when it is brought into contact with the hot fitting and pipe. Be careful not to overheat the fitting and pipe. You can test these by touching the joint with the solder to see if it melts.

As you continue to play the flame over the fitting, bring the end of the solder into contact with the lip of the fitting. When the metal gets hot enough to melt the solder, you will witness the results of a law of nature called capillary action. Not only does the solder melt, it also gets drawn up into the joint under the fitting; this capillary action occurs even when the pipe runs vertically up into the fitting. When the solder begins to flow, remove the flame, and keep applying solder until the entire joint is filled; you know that point is achieved when you see a continuous bead of solder form completely around the lip of the fitting. For neater joints, you can wipe away any excess solder by taking a quick swipe around the fitting lip with a piece of coarse toweling before the solder hardens, but be careful not to touch the hot metal with your hand! Also, be careful not to disturb the soldered joint until the solder has solidified; it could dislodge molten solder and cause leaks.

Caution: The entire process is actually quite simple, but it does demand that you keep some safety precautions clearly in mind. If you are working close to a wall or ceiling, place a scrap of asbestos, gypsum wallboard or a piece of heavy aluminum foil between the pipe and the wall or ceiling. Otherwise, were you accidentally to point the torch in the wrong direction you could char your surroundings or even start a fire. Be especially careful, of course, to keep the flame away from already soldered joints or valves nearby. Wrapping wet rags around good soldered joints and valves is one good

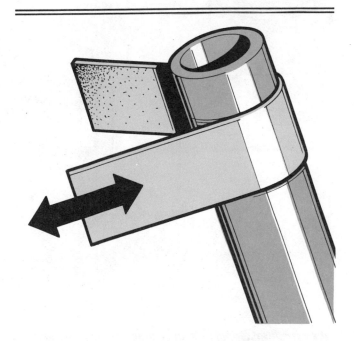

To clean copper pipe before sweat-soldering, wrap an emery cloth strip around the end of the pipe and move it back and forth as if you were buffing a shoe.

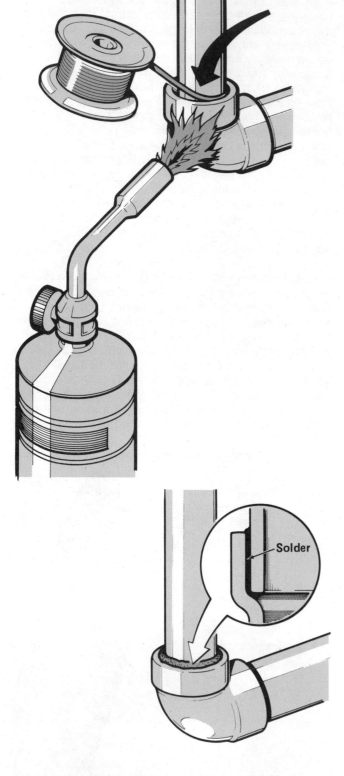

way of dissipating heat and preventing the flame from doing any damage. One other safety rule: When you finish sweat-soldering the joint, turn off the torch immediately.

Many amateur plumbers are so proud of their first sweat-soldered joints that they immediately turn on the water. That, however, is a big mistake. Be sure to allow the joint to cool naturally; the sudden cooling effect of the rushing water can weaken the joint or even cause it to crack. If, when you finally do turn on the water, you discover a leak in the sweat-soldered joint, start the whole job over from scratch: Cut off the water, drain the line, melt the solder, remove the fitting, dry and reclean the fitting, reflux, and finally resolder. There are instances when you can get away without starting over, but it is generally easier, quicker, and more effective to sweat-solder the joint again.

Good sweat-solderers gain their expertise through practice. Therefore, why not buy a few short lengths of copper pipe and some fittings, and try your hand at it before you are faced with a genuine sweat-soldering situation? After you do a few joints, you can be sweat-soldering like a professional.

WORKING WITH GALVANIZED STEEL PIPE

Galvanized steel pipe is pipe that has been treated with zinc to slow corrosion. Despite this zinc treatment, it is still the most corrosion-prone type of pipe used for water supply systems.

Some hardware stores and plumbing supply outlets will cut and thread galvanized pipe for you, if you provide them with the proper sizes you need. Short lengths can be bought in stock sizes already threaded. However, if you plan to cut and thread pipe yourself, you will need some special equipment.

Galvanized steel pipe can be cut with a hacksaw, but a steel pipe cutter — if you have access to one — makes the job much easier.

To cut the pipe with a hacksaw, clamp the length of pipe in a vise that is equipped with a set of pipe jaws, and use a hacksaw with a 24- or 32-tooth-per-inch blade. While cutting, use generous amounts of cutting oil.

To use the pipe cutter, secure the pipe in the vise and clamp the cutter onto the pipe with the cutting wheel on the mark where the cut is to be made. Rotate the cutter completely around the pipe once, then tighten the cutter and rotate the cutter again. Repeat this procedure until the pipe has been cut.

After cutting the pipe, remove the burrs on both the inside and outside end of the pipe. Outside burrs can be removed with a file; inside burrs should be removed with a pipe reamer.

Since galvanized steel pipe is connected with threaded fittings, you must thread the pipe end after each cut. This is done with a pipe die. Install the correct

When sweat-soldering, heat the fitting until it is hot enough to melt the solder and draw it into the joint under the fitting (top). The joint should have a continuous bead of solder completely around it (bottom).

Solder

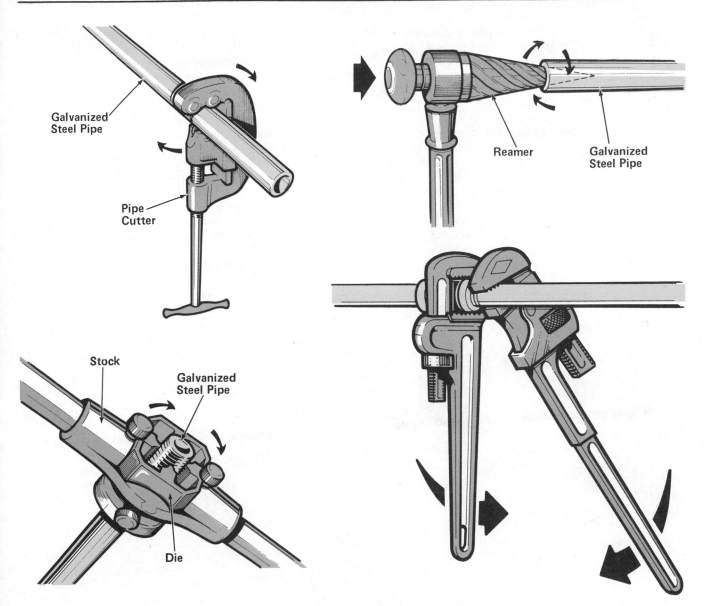

Galvanized steel pipe should be cut with a steel pipe cutter (top, left). Interior burrs are removed with a reamer (top, right), while exterior burrs can be removed with a file. Then, a pipe die is used to cut the threads (bottom, left). Fittings are first hand-tightened, then tightened securely with a pair of pipe wrenches (bottom, right).

size die in the die stock. Then fit the pipe threader and die over the end of the pipe and tighten it. Rotate the stock clockwise, exerting some force at first to start the die-cutting action. Apply generous amounts of cutting oil while cutting the threads. If metal shavings or chips jam the tool, back it off slightly and brush them away. Resume cutting the threads. Stop cutting when the end of the pipe is flush with the die.

When you are ready to join the pipe to its fitting, smear the newly cut threads with pipe joint compound or wrap pipe joint tape around the threads; either method will help seal the completed joint, making it waterproof and leak-free.

Fittings for galvanized steel pipe should be hand-tightened first, and then tightened securely with a pair of pipe wrenches. Apply one wrench to the pipe and one to the fitting. They must be turned in *opposite* directions, with the jaw of each wrench facing the direction in which it is being turned. Tighten the pipe and fitting until there are only about three threads still showing outside the fitting. (If either the pipe or fitting is already installed in a run, then use one wrench to hold that pipe or fitting stationary. Use the second wrench to turn the new fitting or pipe until it is tightened properly. The two wrenches should have their jaws facing in opposite directions.)

WORKING WITH PLASTIC PIPE

Although cutting and connecting galvanized steel pipe is not difficult, it cannot match the ease and convenience of working with plastic pipe. Some plastic pipe can be threaded and connected with threaded fittings, much like galvanized steel pipe; other types of plastic pipe are joined by welding sections together with a chemical solvent. Joining plastic pipe with solvent is almost as simple as gluing photographs in an album. And plastic is a joy to cut as compared to cutting steel pipe.

Plastic pipe can be cut with a plastic-pipe cutter, but any fine-toothed hacksaw can be used. Sawing plastic requires very little effort, and a file or a sharp knife, along with light sanding, can get rid of all the little burrs both inside and outside the cut end. Of course, plastic pipe — like any other type of pipe — must be cut square. To obtain a square cut, it is best to use an inexpensive miter box.

After cutting the pipe, remove the burrs — both inside and out. Then, apply a special cleaner to remove any oil or wax. Next, brush the solvent on the end of the pipe and inside the fitting.

NOTE: Make sure that you use the proper solvent. It is a good idea to purchase the correct cleaner and solvent when you purchase the plastic pipe. Also, avoid using a brush with synthetic bristles to apply the solvent; the solvent will dissolve the synthetic bristles.

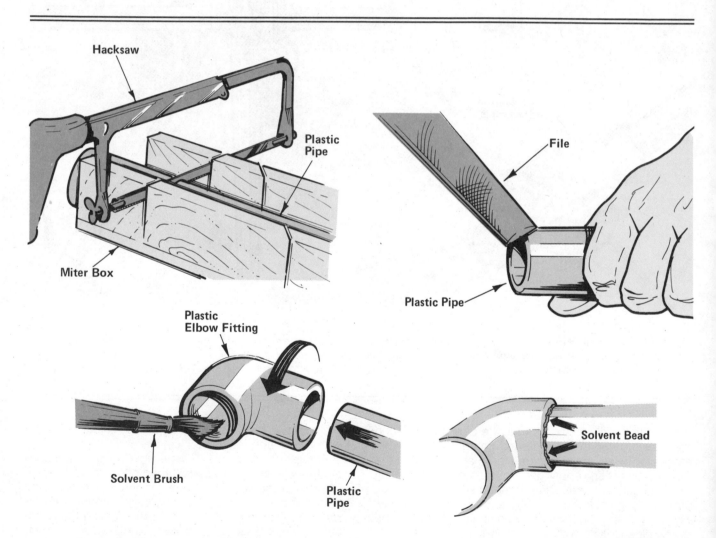

Plastic pipe that is to be solvent-welded should be cut squarely by using a miter box (top, left). Burrs can be removed with a sharp knife or a file (top, right). Solvent is applied to both the fitting and the end of the pipe (bottom, left). Although the solvent sets quickly, the joint (bottom, right) should cure for about 12 hours before testing.

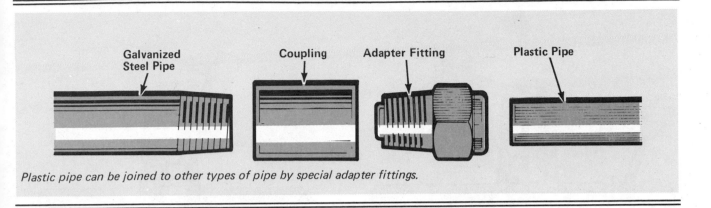

Plastic pipe can be joined to other types of pipe by special adapter fittings.

After applying the solvent to both pieces, insert the end of the pipe into the fitting and twist the pipe a quarter-turn; this distributes the solvent more evenly. Do this, however, quickly and without hesitation, because the solvent goes right to work in forming the bond. It actually welds or fuses the two parts together. Hold the fitting in its correct position for about 15 seconds to prevent any slippage. Clean off any excess solvent.

Despite the fact that the solvent sets quickly, do not turn on the water or otherwise test the solvent-welded joint for about 12 hours.

Some types of plastic pipe, meanwhile, must be connected differently. With PE (polyethylene) pipe, for example, ringed insertion fittings are slipped into the pipe and secured with stainless-steel worm-drive clamps around the outside of the pipe. PB (polybutylene) pipe lengths can be joined in the same manner, but special mechanically gripping transition adapter fittings are most commonly used.

Plastic pipe can be joined — where local codes permit — to other types of pipe by special adapter fittings. For example, suppose you want to use plastic pipe for an underground sprinkler system. At some point, you must attach the plastic pipe to your existing plumbing, which is galvanized steel pipe. You can make the connection easily with an adapter designed specifically for linking plastic to galvanized steel pipes.

WORKING WITH CAST-IRON PIPE

Cast-iron pipe is more difficult to work with than copper, galvanized or plastic pipe. Smart do-it-yourself plumbers always plan ahead when it comes to dealing with cast iron; they try to arrange as few cuts as possible.

If you do not have access to a soil-pipe cutter, follow these steps to cut cast-iron pipe: Draw a line around the pipe with chalk where the cut will be. From this point on, the pipe requires support — it should not rest on the hub. Place the pipe crosswise on a length of 2x4, with the chalk line directly over the wood. Score the pipe with a hacksaw, making a shallow cut all the way around at the chalk mark. Be sure that the cut is

square and that you score the pipe to a depth of about 1/16 inch. Then move the pipe so that the scored line slightly overhangs the 2x4. If you are cutting the lighter service-weight pipe, use a heavy hammer to tap near the cut line on the part of pipe to be removed. Continue to tap gently until the pipe breaks cleanly. If you are cutting the heavier grade of cast-iron pipe, place the tip of a cold chisel in the scored line. Tap the chisel gently with a heavy hammer. Apply the hammer and chisel all the way around the scored line until the pipe breaks.

Cast-iron pipe can be joined using one of three methods: the bell-and-spigot joint, the gasket-type or compression connection, or the no-hub or hubless system.

Bell-and-Spigot Joints

The bell-and-spigot joint is the oldest method of joining cast-iron pipe, and it is still in widespread use. In this type of joint one end of the pipe has a bell-shaped hub into which the slightly ridged end (the spigot) of the connecting pipe fits. You will find that there is space to spare between the two sections of pipe; you caulk this space with a sort of oily rope fiber called oakum. The strands of oakum are wrapped around the pipe, and then are packed down into the gap between the two sections of pipe with a hammer and a tool called a yarning iron. When the oakum fills the void up to about an inch from the edge of the hub (different plumbing codes specify different depths), molten lead is poured over it.

Caution: Before working with molten lead — which can be a hazardous procedure — make sure the pipes you are working on are clean and dry; moisture can cause molten lead to splatter out from the joint and seriously injure you! *Always* wear protective safety goggles and heavy gloves.

The following is the general procedure for joining vertical pipes: First heat the lead. Also heat the ladle; dipping a cold ladle into the lead could cause an explosion. While you are waiting for the lead to melt, pack the oakum into the joint. When the oakum has been packed down firmly to the proper depth to form a solid

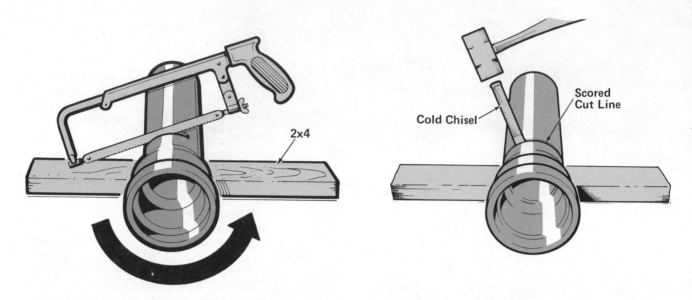

To cut cast-iron pipe, place the pipe section over a length of 2x4 and score the pipe with a hacksaw, making a shallow cut all around it (left). On service-weight pipe, use a heavy hammer to tap near the cut on the piece to be removed; on heavier pipe, use a cold chisel with the hammer (right).

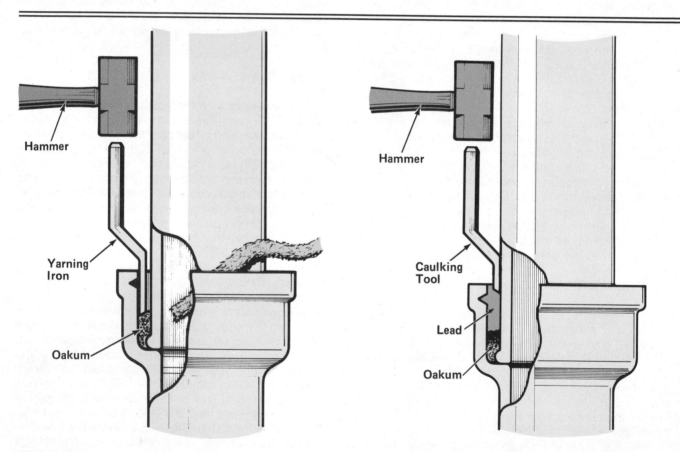

When making bell-and-spigot joints with cast-iron pipe, the joint is packed with oakum, using a hammer and yarning iron (left). Then, the joint is carefully filled with molten lead, which is packed down with a hammer and caulking tool (right).

bed for the lead, carefully and cautiously pour the molten lead into the joint. The lead should be poured continuously and evenly into the joint until the level of the lead is even with the top of the hub.

When the lead cools and begins to harden, tap the lead with a caulking iron and hammer, packing it tight against the bed of oakum and the sides of the joint to make an airtight and leakproof seal. First, work all the way around the inner edge of the joint; then work around the outer edge.

NOTE: This procedure is followed whether you are connecting two sections of cast-iron pipe or a pipe to a fitting. The only time you do anything different is when you are working on a *horizontal* joint. Then you must use a device called an asbestos joint runner to keep the lead from running out of the hub as it is poured.

After the oakum has been packed into the joint, the joint runner is placed around the pipe just above the hub with its clamp at the top; the clamp forms a funnel for pouring the lead. Before pouring, make sure that the joint runner is tightly against the top of the hub so lead does not seep out. After the lead begins to harden, remove the joint runner and begin tapping down the lead in the joint as with vertical joints.

Gasket-Type Fittings

Compression or gasket-type fittings on cast-iron pipe also include a belled hub on one pipe, but the end of the other pipe is hubless. A lubricated neoprene gasket that is inserted into the bell holds the connection together. To make such a connection, the gasket is first fitted into the hub. Then, the hubless section is forced into the gasket to form a leakproof seal. Not all local plumbing codes, however, approve of this type of connection.

No-Hub Joints

The newest and easiest way to join cast-iron pipe is the hubless or no-hub system. In this system, the ends of all the pipes and fittings are plain; they are joined by a neoprene sleeve that is held in place by a gasket or shield and clamps.

To make a hubless connection, the neoprene sleeve is fitted over the end of one pipe, and the gasket and clamps over the other. The ends of the two pipes are aligned and brought together. The sleeve and gasket are then centered over the joint, and the clamps are tightened.

No-hub connections are easy to put together, and they have a definite advantage over other cast-iron connections in that they are easy to take apart. Their only disadvantage — the same one that plagues plastic pipe — is that some local plumbing codes forbid their use. Many codes specifically exclude them from underground installations.

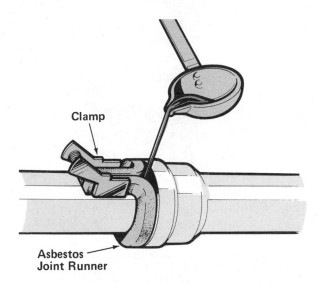

On horizontal joints, an asbestos joint runner is placed around the joint to keep molten lead from running out.

INSTALLING NEW OR REPLACEMENT PIPE

Before you add or change any pipe anywhere in your house, check your local plumbing code to learn what is allowed and what is prohibited, and whether or not a homeowner is allowed to do his own work.

After you have determined that you can proceed, you should realize that installing new plumbing is never easy, but it need not be a nightmare either. There are certain basic ground rules and many useful techniques that any do-it-yourselfer should know before adding or replacing any kind of pipe.

Remember that the drainage lines work on the basis of gravitational pull — not water pressure. Therefore, when you are adding or replacing drainpipes, they must be pitched so that the *downward* flow will carry out the waste. The normal degree of pitch is 1/4 inch per foot.

All runs of pipe must be supported properly — either by hangers, straps, notches cut or holes drilled in the studs or joists, or by whatever method is best for the given situation. If you notch a joist, be sure to compensate for the lost strength by nailing a brace strip under the pipe. This should be a steel brace or a 2x4 about 4 feet long. Notches in studs should be reinforced with metal mending plates. It is always best to run the pipe across the upper half of the studs because the higher the notches the less the studs are weakened. Also, do not notch a joist or stud more than a quarter of its depth. Keep in mind that drilling holes for a pipe run weakens joists or studs *less* than cutting notches does. Again, the diameter of the hole should be less than a quarter of the joist or stud depth.

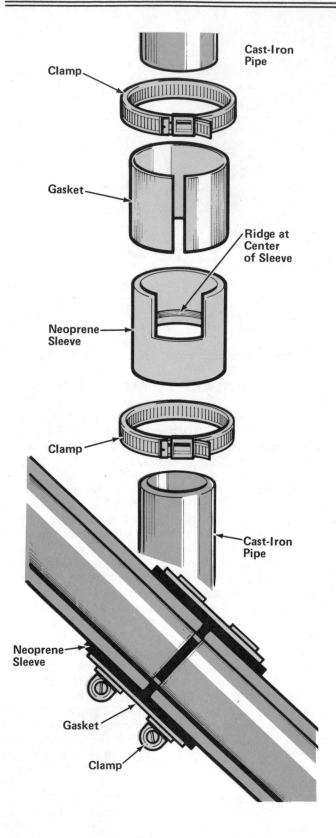

Clamp

Cast-Iron
Pipe

Gasket

Ridge at
Center
of Sleeve

Neoprene
Sleeve

Clamp

Cast-Iron
Pipe

Neoprene
Sleeve

Gasket

Clamp

The no-hub system of joining cast-iron pipe uses a neoprene sleeve that is held in place by a gasket, or shield, and clamps.

Plan the entire run of pipe carefully before you start doing any work whatsoever. If you must tear into floors or walls to correct pipe problems, consider substituting a new run over an entirely different course. Naturally, there are questions of aesthetics, but even running pipe along the outside of an interior wall may — when properly boxed — be preferable to ripping into the walls themselves. Frequently, you can hide a visible stretch of pipe by running it through a closet.

Once you decide exactly how you plan to install your new or replacement pipe, you must know how to order the lengths you will need. To measure pipe properly, you must consider two factors in addition to the length of the pipe you can see: One of these is "fitting gain," or the amount of distance added by the fitting itself. The other is "make-up," or the amount of each end of the pipe that goes into the fitting. Since pipes in most fittings do not butt up against each other, the fitting gain must be added to the length for the overall run and the make-up must be added to the individual sections of pipe. Threaded fittings are so standardized that your hardware or plumbing supply store can show you a table that tells you the screw-in distance; then you should have no problem in measuring the pipes and fittings you plan to install.

With most rigid copper or plastic pipe fittings, you can see from the outside just how much of the pipe goes inside, and with flexible copper or plastic tubing precise measuring is not critical because you can generally make the tubing fit — provided you have sufficient length — with a little gentle bending. Bell-and-spigot connections for cast-iron pipe, however, require that you measure the distance from the bell lip down to the place where the spigot will rest. Since no-hub fittings butt up against each other, there is neither gain nor make-up to consider.

Whenever possible, connections or joints should be kept to a minimum in every run of pipe because each joint represents a possible source for a leak and is a point of flow resistance.

STOPPING LEAKS IN PIPES AND JOINTS

There are all kinds of leaks; some can flood your home, while others are not nearly so damaging. Your approach to stopping a particular leak, therefore, depends on the type of leak it happens to be.

The safest and surest way to repair a leaking pipe is to remove the section that has the leak in it and replace it with a new section. But that is more easily said than done. When you turn a threaded galvanized steel pipe, for instance, to unscrew it from its fitting at one end, you tighten the pipe into its fitting at the other end. There is, of course, a solution to this dilemma; but before going into that, consider another alternative: the pipe patch.

You will find patch kits for plumbing leaks at your

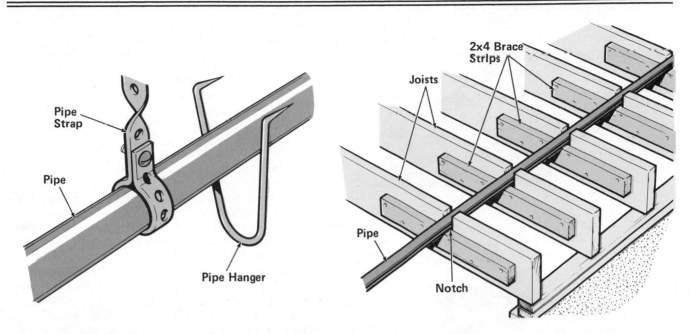

All runs of pipe must be supported properly—either by hangers, straps, notches cut or holes drilled in the studs or joists. If a joist is notched, compensate for the lost strength by nailing a brace strip under the pipe.

local hardware store, or you can rig up your own with a piece of heavy rubber from an old inner tube and a C-clamp. Another possibility is to use a hose clamp with the rubber patch. The factory-made kits generally contain a rubber pad that goes over the hole in the pipe and metal plates that bolt tightly together to compress the rubber pad against the hole in the pipe. The homemade rubber patch and the C-clamp do the same thing, but you may wish to place a block of wood against the pad or cut a tin can along its seam and wrap the can around the rubber patch to spread the clamping pressure better. A quick and easy way to stop a leak, the patch kit can even be used on a permanent basis if the pipe is otherwise sound.

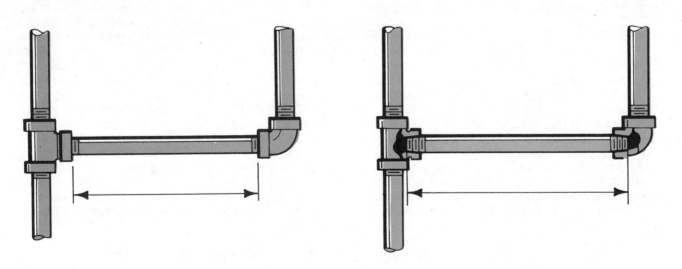

The measure pipe properly, you must consider two factors in addition to the length of the pipe you can see. One is "fitting gain," the amount of distance added by the fitting itself; the other is "make-up," the amount of each end of the pipe that goes into the fitting.

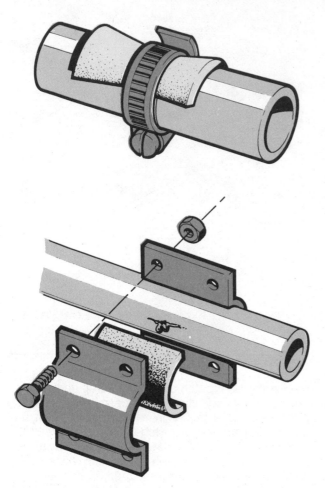

There are several ways to stop a leak in a pipe, including using a piece of heavy rubber and a hose clamp (top), and a rubber pad and two plates that are bolted together (bottom).

Other quick and easy — but temporary — measures for stopping pipe leaks include wrapping waterproof tape over the bad spot and rubbing the hole with a stick of special compound. Applying epoxy paste to the leak or inserting a self-tapping plug into the hole are other alternatives. When using the waterproof tape, be sure to dry the pipe thoroughly before you start wrapping. Then, start the tape about 2 to 3 inches from the hole and extend it the same distance beyond. For tiny leaks in pipes, there is probably no easier cure than the compound sticks that are available at most hardware stores. You just rub the stick over the hole to stop the leak; it can even stop small leaks while the water is still running in the pipe. Epoxy paste can be applied only to dry pipes; and the water must be turned off. The self-tapping plugs are best used only for leaks in large pipes or in tanks; they impede the flow of water in smaller pipes. When tightened down, the screw applies enough pressure to stop the leak.

The problem with these solutions, however, is that a pipe that is bad enough to spring one leak often starts leaking in other locations as well. You may fix one spot, only to see the pipe burst somewhere else. Especially in cases where the leak results from substantial corrosion, the chances are that the whole section of pipe needs replacing.

Replacing Galvanized Steel Pipe

That gets us back to the dilemma of removing the threaded steel pipe that gets tighter at one end when you loosen the other end. The solution to this seemingly impossible situation is to cut the pipe at a point midway between the joints. Before you do any cutting, however, you must turn off the water. In addition, drain all the water out of the system by opening the faucets *below* the pipe or by opening the drain valve that is built into the system. You must also be exceedingly careful in sawing and removing so you do not put undue strain on other parts of the pipe system. Therefore, before sawing, make sure that the pipe is properly braced; the two stubs left by the cut will be heavy, and unless you have them propped up they will sag and pull on the joints. The last thing you want to have happen is for your sawing to break the seal at an otherwise perfect joint in your plumbing system.

Use a fine-toothed, 24- to 32-tooth-per-inch blade in your hacksaw for cutting, and saw right straight through the pipe. Now, by gripping the fitting at one end of the section with one wrench and the cut section of pipe with another, you can turn the pipe stub out of its fitting. Do the same for the other stub section of pipe. Once you remove both stubs you can install the new pipe.

Replace the leaky pipe with two sections of good pipe that are connected by a union fitting. A union fitting has two threaded sections that are pulled together by turning a special nut in the middle of the fitting. A union allows you to fasten the pipes together without having to twist the pipes themselves. Measure the sections of pipe carefully to assure a proper fit, and be sure to add in the length of the union when figuring the overall run of pipe. The two new sections of pipe must be threaded on both ends, and — as is true of all threaded metal connections — the ends should be coated with pipe joint compound or plumber's joint tape to make the joints watertight. To install the two sections of new pipe, screw each of them into its fitting at each end of the run. Then join the sections together with the union fitting.

Replacing Copper Pipe and Tubing

When you must replace a section of soldered copper pipe or tubing, melt the solder in the joints at each end of the section. Remove the old section of pipe; clean the solder out of the fittings. To install the new section of pipe, prepare the fittings and pipe and sweat-solder the joints following the procedures outlined in "Sweat-Soldering" earlier in this chapter.

Caution: Before working on the section, do not forget to turn off the water and drain all the water out of the system by opening the faucets below the pipe or by opening the drain valve that is built into the system. Dry the pipes as thoroughly as you can and stuff balls of white bread into the cut ends to absorb any moisture when you solder.

If there is not enough "give" in the run to allow you to remove an old section of rigid pipe from its fittings in one piece, you can use a tube cutter to sever the pipe midway between the two joints. Then remove the pipe stubs from their fittings. Replace the old pipe with two new sections of pipe connected by a copper-to-copper union fitting.

Replacing Plastic Pipe

If you have a problem with a leaky section of plastic pipe that has been solvent-welded to fittings, you cannot remove the section from its fittings; instead, you must cut the section just *outside* the fittings at each end of the section you plan to replace. First, you must turn off the water, and drain all the water out of the system by opening the faucets *below* the pipe or by opening the drain valve that is built into the system.

Use a fine-toothed hacksaw to cut completely through the plastic pipe outside the two fittings. Now, carefully measure the amount of replacement plastic pipe you will need to replace that section, keeping in mind that the run of pipe will be a bit longer because you have removed the fittings as well. You also will need two new plastic fittings to replace those you have removed, plus a union fitting. To install the new section of pipe, follow the procedure outlined in the section "Working with Plastic Pipe" earlier in this chapter.

Repairing Leaking Joints

What do you do if there is a leak in a joint? That depends on what type of joint it is. If it is a leak in a sweat-soldered joint in copper pipe or tubing, you should melt the solder in the joint, take it apart, clean it, and sweat-solder it all over again. Leaky joints in plastic pipe must be cut out and replaced, because the solvent that fuses pieces of plastic pipe together does such a good job there is no way to get the pieces apart.

A threaded joint in galvanized steel pipe or cast-iron pipe may only need retightening when it starts to leak. Should retightening not stop the leak, however, try applying epoxy paste to the joint. You must, however, first cut off the water, dry the pipe thoroughly, and then follow the directions for applying the epoxy; that should stop the leak.

A union fitting has two threaded sections that are pulled together by turning a nut in the middle of the fitting.

One of the easiest ways to solve a leaking joint problem is to install a nylon type of fitting that requires no solvent, no solder, and no tools. Such fittings are available for use with plastic, copper or other types of metal pipe, and for either hot or cold water service.

SWEATING PIPES

Sometimes you can find so much water dripping from a pipe that you become convinced there must be a leak somewhere. On closer examination, however, you may discover that there is no leak, even though your floors and furnishings suffer as much damage as though there were. What you are witnessing is a natural phenomenon called condensation or "sweating."

Sweating occurs when the water inside the pipe is much colder than the surrounding humid air, a situation that exists nearly the year round in many homes. During summer, the surrounding air is naturally hot, and during the winter the air is heated by the furnace. In either case, when the warm humid air reaches the cold pipes (and the water that comes from below ground is always fairly cool), drops of moisture form and drip down as if there were a tiny hole in the pipe.

One good way to control the moisture problem of a sweating pipe is to insulate the pipes. There are several types of thick "drip" tape in rolls of self-sticking material that will adhere easily to the problem pipes. Before applying the tape, wipe the pipes as dry as you can. Once you wind the tape so that it completely covers the pipe and the fittings, you should see no further signs of sweating.

Another sweat-fighter is an asbestos tape; but you must use it with a special asbestos cement for best results. Soak the tape in the cement until it becomes like *papier-mâché* for molding around odd-shaped fittings. For straight runs of pipe, ready-made asbestos or fiberglass pipe jackets are excellent. There are also no-drip compounds that you can brush on pipe to form a coating of insulation.

It is well worth your time, effort, and expense to eliminate condensation problems. The moisture that drips from sweating pipes can harm your floors, encourage mildew, and cause other damage.

DISASTER LEAKS

Leaks that produce puddles are one thing, but a leak or burst pipe that can flood your home with hundreds of gallons of water is another story altogether. The pressure of the water supply system is so strong that by the time you can call a plumber, a burst pipe can do thousands of dollars in damage to your house and its furnishings.

Plumbing emergencies, however, need not become plumbing disasters. If you take the time now — when there is no water rising in your basement — you can learn how to prevent personal injuries and to limit property damage should a pipe ever spring a serious leak. The first thing to do is to make sure that everyone in the household knows how to shut off the flow of water. The second is to make sure that everyone knows how to shut off the flow of electric current in the house.

The main water shutoff is usually located very close to where the water supply enters your house. It may be a gate valve or it may be an L-shaped rod. If the water meter is in your basement, you could have a valve shutoff that requires a wrench for turning. In any case, find out exactly how the main water shutoff works and — most importantly — if it works. Little-used valves have a way of corroding, and it is much better to find out now that you need a new valve than when you are in a panic situation. As for preventive maintenance, it is always a good idea to turn the water shutoff valve off and on briefly once every six months or so to keep it in working order. Another smart idea is to tag the shutoff with brief instructions or a drawing that indicates how to close the valve.

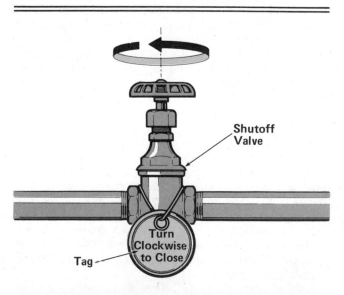

It is a good idea to tag the house's main shutoff so that anyone can find the valve and know which way to turn off the water in an emergency.

It is equally important that everyone in the family know how to throw the master switch that cuts off all the electric current throughout the house. Remember that the flooding water in your house can come in contact with electrical devices and equipment. Make sure that you do not complete the fatal triangle! Any time there is even a remote chance of a water-electricity contact, do not start wading around in the water until the household current has been turned off.

With the water and electrical lines off, you can take your time and calmly evaluate the damage. You can determine whether the pipe that burst is otherwise sound and can function well after patching, or whether you must replace the faulty — and possibly corroded — section with new pipe. If you think that patching will do the job, but do not want to use a rubber pad and clamp patch, consider applying epoxy paste. Just be sure to follow the directions and allow for the full curing time.

A break in a supply line certainly constitutes the worst sort of plumbing emergency, but some people regard an overflowing clogged drainpipe as an emergency situation as well. To take the clogged drain out of the emergency category and into the simple repair category, however, all you need do is to make sure that no additional water enters the drain until you can clear it. This, nevertheless, can often be a tricky assignment. Frequently, one section of drain serves several outlets, and you must make certain that no water flows into any of them until you remove the clog. It is a good idea to shut off the water supply stop valves at fixtures served by the clogged drain.

THAWING FROZEN PIPES

You may think that your entire plumbing system is in perfect working order and that there is little or no chance of a pipe bursting and flooding your house. Yet there is one situation that you may not have considered. Water that freezes during winter in an unprotected pipe expands, and that expansion can rupture an otherwise sound pipe. Of course, a frozen pipe is always an inconvenience, but it can result in a much more serious situation than just a temporary loss of water.

If ever there were an example of how a little prevention is superior to a lot of cure, fighting frozen pipes is it. By taking the proper preventive steps, you may never need to worry about thawing frozen pipes — or worse yet — repairing a pipe that ruptures when the water in it freezes solid.

If you are building a new house or adding pipes underground, follow these freeze-fighting tips. Bury the pipes *below* the frost line. Since this depth varies in different regions, check with your local National Weather Service office to learn about the frost line in your community. Make sure that the new pipes are as well-insulated as is practical, and run as many pipes as you can along your home's inner walls instead of along its outside walls. If you have pipes on outside walls leading to outside faucets, make sure that the faucets are the frost-free type. When cold weather sets in, shut off the water to the outside faucets and open the faucet to drain the exposed pipe. Finally, if you know that you have a stretch of pipe that is subject to freezing, wrap the pipe with heat tape (sometimes called heat cable) or pipe insulation. You can purchase heat tape that has an automatic thermostat to start the heat when the outside temperature drops to about 38°F.

What happens, though, when you wake up some frigid winter morning to find a water pipe frozen solid? What you need then are not freeze-fighting tips, but rather directions on the best way to thaw frozen pipes.

Before doing anything else, open the faucet so that the steam produced by your thawing activities will be able to escape. In addition, start thawing the pipe at the faucet and work back toward the other end of the frozen section. As you melt the ice, the water and steam will come out the open faucet; if you were to start in the middle, the steam produced by the melting ice could get trapped and build up enough pressure to rupture the pipe.

You can use any of several pipe-thawing heat sources. Probably the most popular — and certainly the safest — is hot water. Wrap and secure a heavy towel or a burlap bag around the pipe to concentrate and hold the heat against the pipe. Pour the hottest water you can obtain over the towel, but be careful because most of the water will run off of the towel onto you or the floor. A properly positioned bucket can save you both a scalding and a mess.

A less messy but far more dangerous heat source for thawing frozen pipes is a propane torch equipped with a flame-spreader nozzle. However, you must be extremely careful to prevent the torch flame from damaging or igniting the wall behind the pipe. A scrap of asbestos siding or some other fireproof material between the pipe and the wall is a good precautionary measure, but the way you use the torch is the main ingredient in safe pipe thawing. Keep the flame moving back and forth; never leave it very long in one spot. Be especially careful if you are near any soldered pipe joints. Pass over them very quickly or they may melt and cause leaks, and you will find that you have a much more serious plumbing problem on your hands than a frozen pipe. Never use a torch or other direct high heat on plastic pipe.

If you want to avoid the messiness of thawing with hot water and the danger of melting soldered joints with a propane torch, you can use a heat lamp, a hair dryer or an electric iron as the heat source. They are slower-working, but safer to use.

There is a special technique for thawing a frozen drainpipe. Actually, all it involves is melting the blockage with hot water; but if the ice is some distance from

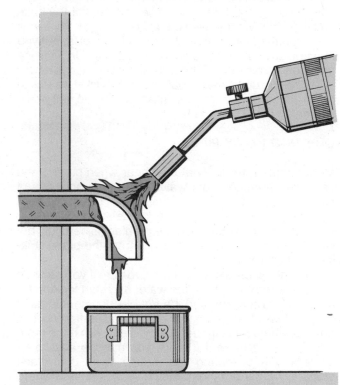

Two methods of thawing a frozen pipe are pouring hot water over rags wrapped around the pipe (top), and using a propane torch (bottom). Use care with a torch; keep the flame moving and place asbestos to protect walls.

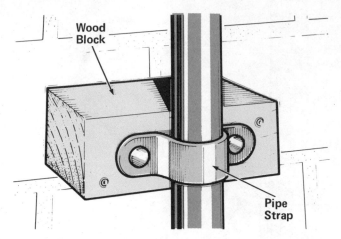

Wood Block

Pipe Strap

A pipe banging against a masonry wall can be silenced by wedging a wood block behind it, fastening the block to the wall, and securing the pipe to the wood with a pipe strap.

the drain opening, the hot water you pour in could cool considerably before it reaches the trouble spot. Therefore, in such cases you should remove the trap and insert a length of garden hose into the drainpipe. When the hose reaches the ice — that is, when you cannot push it along any further — raise your end of the hose and feed hot water in with the aid of a funnel. This way, the hot water is sure to get to the problem area; but you must be careful when using this technique. Until the ice melts and drains down the pipe, the hot water you pour in will back up toward you. Have a bucket ready to catch the overflow, and be alert so you do not scald yourself.

QUIETING NOISY PIPES

Most people refer to what they hear when pipes bang as "water hammer," but water hammer is only one of several different mysterious noises that can come from your plumbing system. If you hear the sound whenever you turn on the water, then the problem is certainly not water hammer; it probably results from the pipes striking against something.

Banging pipes are much easier to cure if you can see them. Therefore, turn on the water and start looking for movement; once you find the trouble, you should have no problem in stopping the pipe or pipes from hitting against whatever is in the vicinity. Yet, even if the moving pipe is between the walls, you may be able to silence it without tearing your house apart. Just place stops — rubber or other padding — at each end where the pipe emerges from behind the wall.

Generally, you will find that the moving pipe is loose within its strap or U-clamp, and is banging against the wall to which it is supposed to be secured. To eliminate the noise completely, just slit a piece of old garden

hose or cut a patch of rubber and insert it in the strap or clamp to fill in the gap. Pipes that strike against a masonry wall can be silenced by wedging a block of wood between the pipe and the wall. Then, nail the block to the wall with masonry nails — or with a screw installed in a masonry wall anchor — and attach the pipe to the block with a pipe strap.

In a basement or crawl space, you will frequently find galvanized steel pipes suspended from the joists by perforated pipe straps. While this is a perfectly proper installation, a long run of suspended pipe can move within the straps, strike against something, and create a racket. A block of wood strategically wedged along the run can eliminate the pipe's movement and, of course, the noise. Whenever you secure a pipe, however, you must be careful not to anchor it so as to restrict its ability to expand and contract with changes in temperature. If you place a bracket on a pipe, be sure to include a rubber buffer between the pipe and the bracket. You can make such buffers from garden hose, radiator hose, foam rubber, rubber cut from old inner tubes or even kitchen sponges.

You may find that supply pipes and drain pipes that run right next to each other are striking one another and creating a clatter. One solution to this problem is to solder — if possible — the two pipes together; another is to wedge a piece of rubber between them. Or, since such vibrations and noises are often caused by water pressure that is too high, you can try reducing the water pressure.

If the knocking sound occurs only when you turn on the hot water, it means that the water heater is set too high; the noise is steam rumbling throughout your hot water system. Try turning the heat setting down in order to silence the pipes.

Pipe that is either too small to begin with or that has become restricted with scale or mineral deposits can be a big noise problem. It is almost impossible to clean clogged supply pipes (a water filter can sometimes prevent such clogging), and you must replace pipe that is too small if you want to stop the noise. On the other hand, you can diminish the sound level of clogged pipes considerably by wrapping them with sound-damping insulation.

Drainpipes rarely clatter, but they can emit a sucking sound as the water leaves the sink or basin. Such a sound means that a vent is restricted or, perhaps, that there is no vent at all attached to the drain. In either case, you have a potentially serious plumbing problem on your hands — not because of the noise, but because a nonfunctioning or nonexistent vent could result in the water seal getting siphoned from the fixture's trap, allowing sewer gas to back up into your home. Run a plumber's snake through the vent from the fixture if possible, or from the roof vent to eliminate any clogging; but if there is no vent on the drain, install an antisiphon trap (available at your hardware store) to quiet the noise and to prevent any problem with sewer gas.

Water hammer is a particular type of plumbing noise, not a generic name for any kind of pipe clatter. It occurs when you shut off the water suddenly, and the force of the fast-moving water rushing through the pipe is brought to a quick halt — creating a sort of shock wave and a hammering noise. Plumbing that is properly installed possesses air chambers or "cushions" that compress when the shock wave hits, softening the blow and preventing any hammering. The chambers can fail, though, because water under pressure gradually absorbs the air. If you had formerly experienced no hammering and then it suddenly started, most likely your plumbing system's air chambers became waterlogged.

You can cure water hammer by cutting off the water behind the waterlogged chambers (perhaps even at the main shutoff), opening the offending faucet, and permitting the faucet to drain thoroughly. Once all the water drains from the chamber, air will go back in, fill up the chamber, and restore the cushion. If the air chamber is located below the outlet, you may have to drain the main supply lines to allow the chamber to fill with air again.

The air chamber will not drain properly if it is clogged with scale or residue from chemicals in the water. The chamber should be a bit larger than the supply pipe to which it is attached to preclude such clogging. Since the chamber is merely a capped length of pipe, however, all you have to do to clear it is remove the cap and ream out the scale.

What do you do, however, if there are no air chambers built into your plumbing system? You must do something, because water hammer pressures are often sufficient to cause eventual damage — failure of fittings or burst pipes. The problem is most often caused by water pressure that is too high, so the first step is to reduce the water pressure if possible. Sometimes this is not feasible, because a reduction in pressure may result in only a dribble of water available at an upper-floor faucet if another on the first floor is turned on. Where the idea is a workable one, you can reduce pressure by installing a pressure-reducing valve in the supply line that comes into the house. The same purpose is served by installing a globe valve (a valve that halts water flow with a washer) at the head of the affected pipeline, but this also may result in pressure too low for proper operation of the fixtures on the line when other faucets are open. If pressure reduction is unfeasible or ineffective, you must install the necessary air chambers to prevent water hammer. If you have no room to make the installation (without tearing into a wall), go to your plumbing supply dealer and find out about the substitute devices that are designed for such problem areas. Many of these devices have a valve that makes it easy for air to re-enter the system.

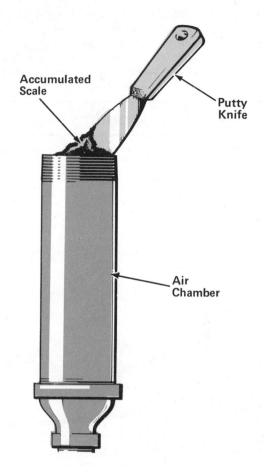

An air chamber will not drain properly if it is clogged. Remove its cap and ream out the accumulated scale inside.

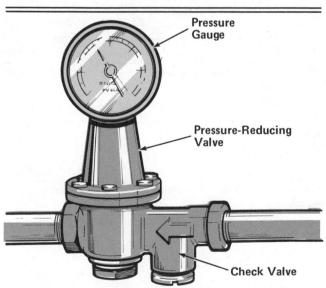

If you must reduce the water pressure in your home's plumbing system, a pressure-reducing valve can be installed in the supply pipe coming into the house.

If you are adding new plumbing, make sure that the pipes are big enough to allow the water to flow properly. Often, the minimum size acceptable to your local plumbing code turns out to be unacceptable to you when you hear it clatter. Remember to keep the air chambers in good working order and to run pipes in such a way as to prevent their striking each other or nearby walls. If you follow these simple procedures, you should be able to cure most plumbing noises before you hear them.

Pipe Trouble-Shooting Chart

PROBLEMS	CAUSES	REPAIRS
Leaking pipe	1. Joint not watertight.	1. Tighten threaded joint, if possible. Apply epoxy paste to joint. Disassemble and resolder sweat-soldered joint in copper pipe or tubing. Cut out and replace joint in plastic pipe.
	2. Hole in pipe.	2. Repair by patching hole using best available method, or replace section of pipe. If section is inaccessible, disconnect it from system and route new section of pipe.
	3. Burst pipe.	3. Immediately turn off water at main shutoff. Repair or replace pipe or joint. Avoid electrical shock due to contact between electrical devices and equipment and water.
Pipe drips water, but there is no leak	1. Condensation.	1. Apply insulation to pipe.
Noise in pipes—hot water only	1. Steam causing rumbling in hot water pipes.	1. Turn down thermostat setting on water heater or replace faulty thermostat.
	2. Pipe creaks against surroundings from expansion and contraction.	2. Rehang pipe on slip hangers or in larger notches or holes.
Water makes sucking noise when draining	1. Improper venting.	1. Clean roof vent. Add antisiphon trap if there is no vent.
Hammering noise when water is shut off	1. Air chambers waterlogged.	1. Shut off and drain supply line to allow air to reenter air chambers.
	2. No air chamber.	2. Install air chamber.
Banging noise while water is running	1. Loose pipe.	1. Track down loose pipe and brace, cushion or strap it.
No water supply	1. Frozen pipes.	1. Open faucets. Start thawing at closest point to faucet and work back.
	2. Main shutoff valve closed.	2. Open main shutoff valve.
	3. Broken or closed main.	3. Call water department.
	4. Well pump failure.	4. Check and repair pump.

Toilets

The toilet is one of the most important fixtures in your home. Although toilets are — if not maltreated in any way — sturdy and reliable components of the plumbing system, it is a rare homeowner or apartment-dweller who never has any problems with a toilet. Clogging is, perhaps, the most serious toilet trouble, but it is far from the only one. The tank, for example, can make all sorts of strange noises, or it can run water continuously. The toilet bowl can crack, or you may spot leaks around the base where the fixture rests on the floor. Fortunately, most toilet troubles can be fixed by any well-informed do-it-yourselfer.

REPLACING A TOILET SEAT

Undoubtedly, the easiest toilet repair task is replacing the lid and seat. There are so many styles of replacement seats available that you should encounter no difficulty in finding one to match any bathroom color scheme or motif. Most modern toilets are manufactured in two standard sizes, and replacement seats are made to fit them. If your toilet is extra wide or very old, however, you may not be able to use one of the standard replacement seats. In such instances, you may have to place a special order for the seat with a company that deals in plumbing fixtures.

Once you have the right size seat, you must remove the old one. Removal sounds simple. All you have to do is remove two nuts and lift your old toilet seat up and out. You may ask, "What is so difficult in doing that?" Wait until you try to loosen those nuts. Consider yourself among the luckiest of individuals if the nuts that secure your toilet seat are not rusted or corroded; sometimes, in fact, they are recessed and practically inaccessible.

If you can get to the fasteners relatively easily, apply some penetrating oil to help loosen them. Give the oil plenty of time to soak in, and then be sure that you do not use too much force if they are still stubborn. Were the wrench to slip off a stubborn nut, it could strike and crack the tank or the bowl or anything else it happened to hit. If the nuts cannot be reached with a regular wrench, try a deep socket wrench.

When all else fails, you will have to cut off the bolts with a hacksaw. To protect the bowl's finish, apply tape to the bowl at the spots the hacksaw blade is likely to rub against. Then insert the blade under the hinge, and saw through the bolts. Sawing is, however, a measure of last resort; try every other procedure to loosen the nuts first. Then, if you are convinced that nothing is going to break the nuts loose, be extremely cautious in using the saw. A careless slip with a hacksaw can crack the fixture just as a wrench that comes flying off a stubborn nut can crack it.

With the nuts removed or the bolts cut, you can remove the old seat without further difficulty. Clean the area before installing the new seat. The new one can be fastened simply by inserting the bolts and tightening the nuts; but be careful not to overtighten the nuts — you may want to replace this seat too some day. If you live in an apartment and put on a new seat, be sure to keep the old one. When you are ready to leave, you can replace the new one with the original and take your new seat to your new dwelling.

If the toilet lid and seat are still in good condition, but

A new toilet seat can be installed by inserting the two bolts, slipping on the washers, and tightening the nuts.

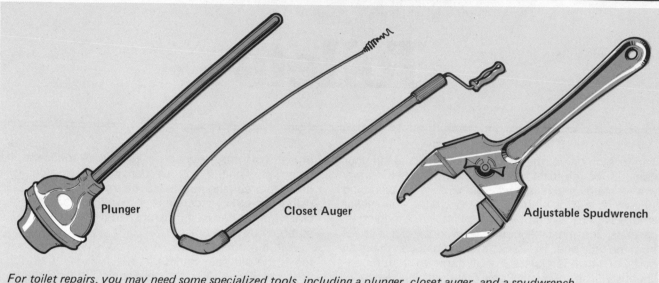

For toilet repairs, you may need some specialized tools, including a plunger, closet auger, and a spudwrench.

the small rubber bumpers on the bottom are in poor condition, you can buy replacements at your local hardware store. Some bumpers screw in, while others require that you nail them in place. Whichever type you have, try to install the new ones in holes that are close enough to conceal the original holes.

SPECIALIZED TOOLS

Few special tools are required for changing a toilet seat: a wrench, or perhaps a deep socket wrench, or hacksaw. Of course, the most frequently used toilet tool is the plumber's friend, also known as a plunger, or force cup or pump. Get one with a long handle, and be sure that the suction cup is large enough to cover the toilet's drain opening.

A closet auger is a version of the plumber's snake, but it is designed specifically for clearing clogs in toilets. The closet auger is shorter than a regular snake, and it comes encased in a metal housing with a crank.

If you really plan to get involved in plumbing chores and you decide to remove a toilet either for replacement or repairs, you may well need a spudwrench. Older toilets frequently have a large pipe that connects the tank to the bowl; this pipe is called a spud, and it is held to the bowl and tank by slip nuts. A spudwrench is designed to remove these extra-large hexagonal slip nuts. The adjustable type of spudwrench is far more versatile than the nonadjustable type, which has a fixed opening of different sizes at each end.

CLEARING A CLOGGED TOILET

You can generally clear a clogged toilet with the plumber's friend, or plunger. Just make sure that there is enough water in the toilet bowl to cover the rubber suction cup, and then work the handle of the plunger up and down. There are two types of plungers, and the one with a bulb-type head is especially effective. Some types have a fold-out head that is designed for toilet use. If there is not enough water in the bowl, do not flush the toilet; flushing a clogged toilet will just cause the bowl to overflow. Instead, bring a pan or pot of water from another source to supply the water you need to cover the plunger cup.

Usually, whatever is blocking the toilet drain is not very far away. If the plunger's action does not dislodge the clog, you can try to hook the blockage and pull it free. A wire coat hanger sometimes can do the job. The coat hanger, however, is really a substitute for the closet or toilet auger. This tool has a long sleeve or tube to guide the snake and auger hook into the trap. A crank on the end enables you to turn the hook in the drain or trap.

Insert the auger in the toilet trap and turn the crank until it feels tight. This means that the snake has twisted its way to and into the blockage. Pull in the auger and you should be able to remove whatever is clogging the toilet. If you are not successful at first, try the closet auger several more times. In some cases, you may have to resort to pushing a regular plumber's snake through the blockage if you are unsuccessful in pulling it out with the auger.

When all else fails, you may have to remove the toilet from the floor and turn it upside down to get at the blockage. Naturally, you should give all the other methods as much opportunity as possible before you actually remove the toilet; this is not what anyone would call an easy task. But neither is it, however, beyond the capabilities of the average do-it-yourselfer, and we will explain exactly how to do the job later in this

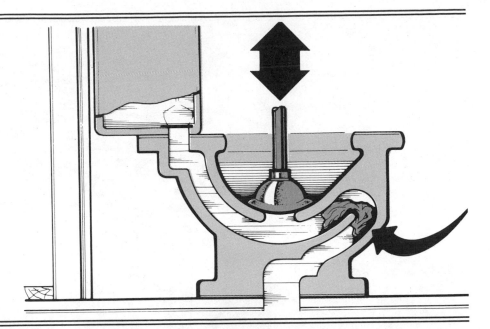

Before using the plunger, make sure there is enough water in the toilet bowl to cover the suction cup.

chapter in the section "Removing and Replacing a Toilet."

TOILET TANK TROUBLES

Compared with a clogged toilet, tank troubles can seem relatively insignificant. Yet these troubles — such as strange noises or water running continuously — can be more than annoying; they can also be costing you money in wasted water. Fortunately, you can eliminate most toilet tank troubles quickly and easily.

Do you ever wonder exactly how a toilet works — what happens between the time that you operate the handle and the time that the toilet is ready for further use? Before you can solve the problems that plague your toilet, you must know exactly how this fixture operates. Here is what typically happens:

When you trip the handle on the tank to flush the toilet, a trip lever is raised inside the tank. This lever lifts wires which, in turn, raise the tank ball (or rubber flap) at the flush valve opening at the bottom of the tank.

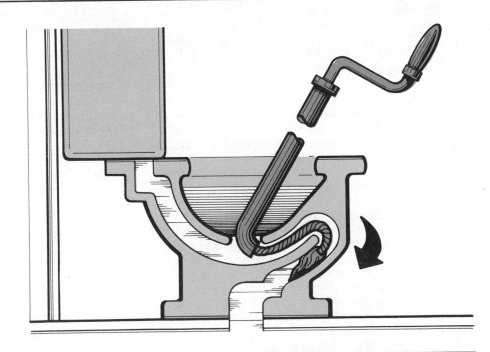

The closet auger has a long sleeve to guide the snake and auger hook into the trap. A crank enables you to turn the hook and free the blockage.

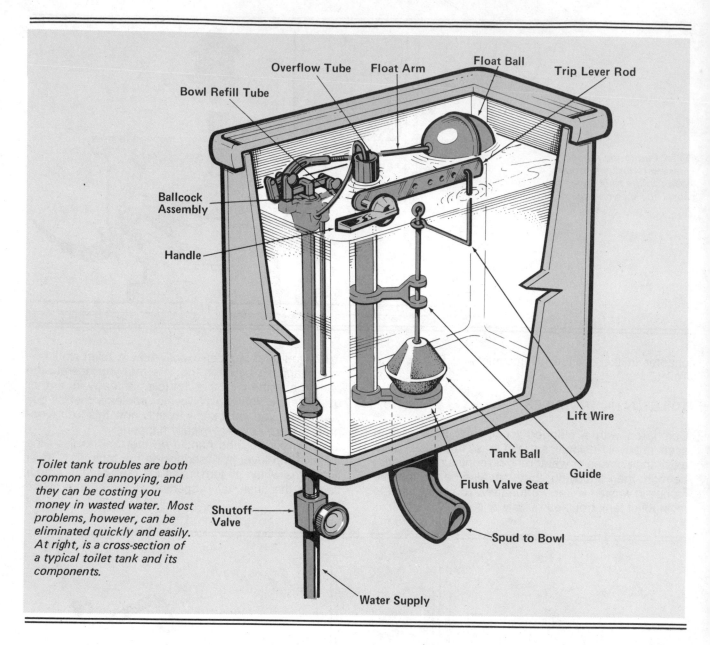

Overflow Tube Float Arm Float Ball Trip Lever Rod

Bowl Refill Tube

Ballcock
Assembly

Handle

Lift Wire

Tank Ball Guide

Flush Valve Seat

*Toilet tank troubles are both
common and annoying, and
they can be costing you
money in wasted water. Most
problems, however, can be
eliminated quickly and easily.
At right, is a cross-section of
a typical toilet tank and its
components.*

Shutoff
Valve

Spud to Bowl

Water Supply

The action causes the water in the tank to rush out past the raised tank ball and into the toilet bowl below. This raises the level of water in the bowl above that of the water in the toilet drain spout. Since water seeks its own level, the water from the tank pushes the bowl water out into the drain, causing a siphoning action that cleans everything out of the bowl. When all the water is gone from the toilet bowl and air is drawn into the drain spout, the siphoning stops.

Meanwhile, the tank ball falls back into place, covering the flush valve opening at the bottom of the tank. In addition, while the water was rushing out of the tank, the float ball, which floats on top of the water in the tank, drops down. This pulls down on the float arm, raising the valve plunger in the ballcock assembly and allowing fresh water to flow into the tank.

As the water level rises in the tank, the float ball rises until the float arm is high enough to lower the valve plunger in the ballcock assembly and shut off the incoming water. If, for some reason, the water should fail to shut off, there is an overflow tube that carries excess water down into the bowl to prevent the tank from overflowing.

Lift the lid off your toilet tank, and you should be able to follow this procedure quite easily. Once you know how the toilet works, you can start to search for the source of toilet tank troubles.

Suppose that your toilet never stops running — water flows continuously out of the tank to the bowl and down the drain. What should you do? Try lifting up on the float arm. If the water stops, you know the problem is that the float ball does not rise far enough to lower the valve plunger in the ballcock assembly. One reason could be that the float ball is rubbing against the side of the tank. If this is the case, bend the float arm slightly to move the ball away from the side.

The problem also could be in the float ball itself. If the ball does not touch the tank, continue to hold the float arm and remove the ball from the end of the arm by turning it counterclockwise. Then shake the ball to see if there is water inside; the weight of water inside could be preventing the ball from rising normally. If there is no water, put the old ball back on and bend the float rod down — very gently — to lower the level that the float ball must reach to shut off the flow of fresh water into the tank.

What do you do if, when you lift the float arm, the water does not stop running? You know then, of course, that the problem is not in the float arm at all. The next logical place to check for trouble is the tank ball at the flush valve seat. Frequently, chemical residue from the water can prevent this ball from seating properly, or the ball itself may have decayed. In either case, the result is the same — water will seep through the flush valve opening into the toilet bowl below.

Turn off the water at the toilet shutoff valve, and flush the toilet to empty the tank. You can now examine the tank ball for signs of wear, and install a new ball if necessary. If the problem is chemical residue on the lip of the flush valve opening, take some wet-dry emery paper, steel wool or even a knife and clean away the debris. You can retard any further formation of such residue by depositing slivers of soap in the tank.

There are still other possible causes for a toilet running continuously. The guide or the lift wires that raise and lower the tank ball may be out of line or bent. Make sure that the guide is in place so that the wires are directly above the flush valve opening. Rotate the guide until the tank ball falls straight down into the opening. If a lift wire is bent, try to bend it back to the correct position or install a new one. Make sure that the trip lever rod is not rubbing against anything and that the lift wire is not installed in the wrong hole of the rod; either situation could cause the tank ball to fall at an angle and not block the opening as it should. If neither the float ball nor the tank ball is at fault, then the problem must be in the ballcock assembly.

WORKING WITH THE BALLCOCK ASSEMBLY

The ballcock assembly looks far more complicated than it really is. Just make sure that the water shutoff valve for the toilet is in the off position, and you are ready to go to work. With many ballcock assemblies, you will find a pair of thumbscrews that hold the valve plunger; but if the unit in your toilet tank has a different linkage arrangement, you still should be able to determine how to remove the valve plunger.

Remove the valve plunger, and you will see one or

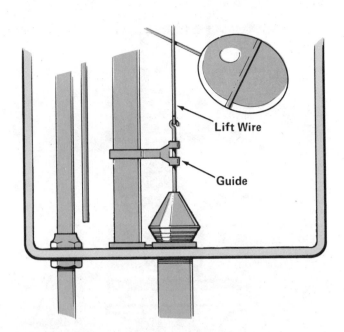

Lift Wire

Guide

If your toilet runs continuously, check the guide and lift wires that raise and lower the tank ball to be sure they are aligned properly.

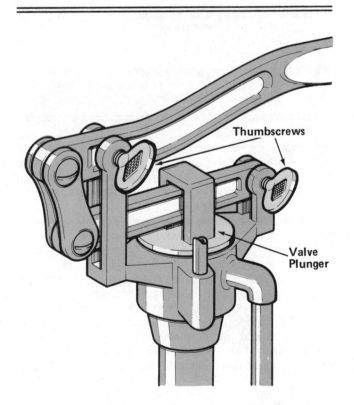

Thumbscrews

Valve Plunger

On many ballcock assemblies, there are a pair of thumbscrews that hold the valve plunger. You will have to unscrew them to remove the valve.

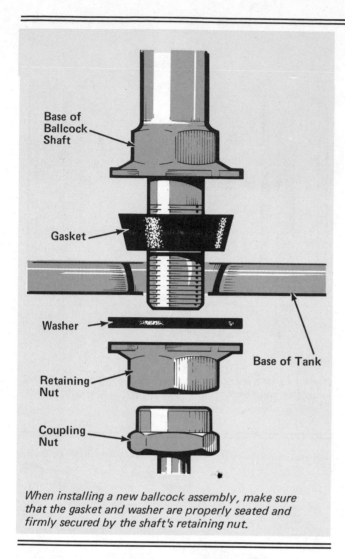

Base of
Ballcock
Shaft

Gasket

Washer

Base of Tank

Retaining
Nut

Coupling
Nut

When installing a new ballcock assembly, make sure that the gasket and washer are properly seated and firmly secured by the shaft's retaining nut.

the tank. Loosen the coupling nut to free the water inlet pipe. Then apply an adjustable wrench to the retaining or locknut immediately above the slip nut under the tank, and another wrench to the base of the ballcock assembly shaft inside the tank. Unscrew the locknut under the tank to remove the ballcock assembly. If the nut is stubborn, try using some penetrating oil to loosen the connection. Lift the old assembly out of the tank, but be sure to save all the washers from all connections both inside and outside the tank. You may not need them — most likely all necessary washers will be included with the replacement unit — but it is always smart to keep the old parts until you install the new ballcock assembly.

Insert the new ballcock assembly in the hole in the tank with the inside washer in place. Tighten the locknut on the outside sufficiently to make the inside washer fit watertight against the hole, but do not over-tighten it. Replace the coupling nut and water inlet pipe, reinstall the float arm, place the refill tube in the overflow tube, and the job is done. Turn the water back on at the toilet shutoff valve, and check for leaks at all joints. Of course, another thing to check is that the float ball does not rub against the back of the tank.

When you go to a hardware or plumbing supply store to purchase a new ballcock assembly, you will find that plastic and metal units are available. Plastic costs less and will not corrode, but plastic assemblies are not as sturdy as metal ones. In addition, plastic units usually cannot be repaired because many of them are sealed. Nevertheless, you can purchase a different type of unit than the one you are replacing so long as the new assembly has a threaded shank the same size as the old one. If possible, bring the old assembly with you when you go to purchase the replacement.

Newer types of ballcock assemblies eliminate the float arm and the float ball. One kind features a plastic cup that floats up to cut off the water as the tank fills with water. You can set the water level in the tank by adjusting the position of the plastic cup on a pull rod. One advantage of this type of ballcock assembly is that it lets the water run full force until the tank is filled; then it shuts the water off immediately, eliminating any groaning noises that some toilets emit as their conventional float arms gradually close the valve.

Another type also eliminates the float ball and float arm. This is a small unit that rests almost on the bottom of the tank, and its diaphragm-powered valve senses the level of the water from down there. Moreover, since it requires no tools, the assembly is an easy unit to install. You may need a couple of common tools for the removal of the old assembly. Here is how the new unit is installed:

The first step is to turn off the tank's water supply shutoff valve. Then, flush the toilet to drain the tank. Sponge up any water remaining in the tank before proceeding. Remove the old ballcock assembly following

two washers — sometimes you will find an O-ring. Naturally, if any of these parts are faulty, water will flow out past the plunger continuously and the toilet will run without ceasing. Examine all of the washers, and replace any defective ones.

Some ballcock assemblies are completely sealed, however, and there is no way that you can get inside the unit without breaking it. If that is what you find when you lift the lid off the toilet tank, you must buy a replacement ballcock assembly. Most cost only a few dollars. Should you discover either a sealed ballcock assembly or a damaged one, the first thing to do is to get all the water out of the tank so that you can remove the old unit and install a new one. Shut off the toilet water supply at the shutoff valve; flush the tank. Use a large sponge to remove whatever water remains inside the tank. Unscrew the float arm from the old ballcock unit, and remove the refill tube from the overflow tube (the refill tube may be clipped on or bent into position).

Now, look under the tank. You will see a coupling or slip nut where the water inlet pipe enters the base of the procedure outlined earlier in this section. Slip the following parts over the water inlet pipe under the tank: coupling nut, friction washer, cone washer, and retaining or mounting nut.

Now, install the new unit inside the tank, fitting the threaded shank down through the hole over the water supply pipe and making certain the gasket fits into the hole. Start the retaining or mounting nut under the tank onto the threaded shank. Hand-tighten it only. Push the washers into place, and hand-tighten the coupling nut under the tank.

Inside the tank, attach one end of the refill tube to the tank's overflow pipe, and place the other end on the stem of the replacement unit. Open the water supply valve to fill the tank. The water level in the tank can be adjusted by a knob on the new valve unit.

INADEQUATE FLUSHING, SWEATING, AND OTHER PROBLEMS

What can you do if too little water comes from the tank to flush the toilet bowl clean? The first thing you should check is the water level in the tank; it is probably too low. If the water level fails to reach within 1½ inches from the top of the overflow tube, try bending the float arm up slightly to allow more water to enter the tank.

In some cases, the water level may be correct, but there still is an insufficient amount of water coming from the tank to clean the bowl properly. Most likely, the culprit in this situation is the tank ball at the flush valve seat at the bottom of the tank. The ball is probably dropping too soon because the guide is set too low. Try raising the guide, but make sure that it stays in line with the lift wires. (If the guide and the wires are out of alignment, then the tank ball will not drop straight into the valve seat opening, and you will find that you have a toilet that runs continuously.)

There is one other possible cause for inadequate flushing. The small ports around the underside of the toilet bowl's rim can get clogged with residue from chemicals in the water and prevent a sufficient amount of tank water from running out into the bowl. A small mirror can help you examine the holes, and a piece of wire coat hanger or an offset Phillips screwdriver — if one is available — can ream out any clogged debris.

Toilet tanks can sweat and drip onto your floors just as pipes can. There are jackets that are designed specifically to fit over the tank and to absorb the moisture. There are also drip pans that fit under the tank to catch and collect the dripping condensation so that it does not damage your bathroom floor. A device, called a temperator valve, is another way to combat tank sweating. The valve provides a regulated mixture of hot and cold water, which lessens the difference between the temperature inside the tank and the temperature of the surrounding air. It is that temperature difference, of course, that causes condensation — or sweating. You

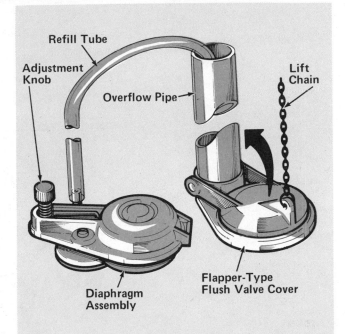

One type of diaphragm-powered valve rests close to the bottom of the tank. It eliminates the float ball and float arm. The tank's water level can be adjusted by a knob on the valve unit.

might consider such a device if the water in the tank is usually below 50°F.

A temperator valve requires you to hook up a hot water line to the valve, which may be quite inconvenient if there is no such line relatively close to the toilet. Moreover, the temperator valve does not prevent the water inside the tank from cooling between flushings; thus, condensation can still occur even on a temperator-equipped toilet.

If you do have an accessible hot water line at a lavatory near the toilet, follow this procedure to install a temperator valve: Turn off the water at the main shutoff. Working at the toilet, drain the tank, disconnect the water inlet pipe from the fixture's shutoff valve, and unscrew the valve from the cold-water supply pipe. Attach the "cold" inlet of the temperator valve to the cold-water supply pipe. Screw a short threaded nipple into the temperator valve outlet; the fixture's shutoff valve is screwed onto the other end of the threaded nipple. Reconnect the toilet tank's water inlet pipe to the shutoff valve.

Now, at the lavatory, disconnect the flexible hot water line leading to the fixture's hot water faucet from the shutoff valve. Install a compression T-fitting with a takeoff adapter in this flexible line. Then reconnect the line, with its T-fitting, to the hot water shutoff valve. Run flexible copper tubing from the T-fitting to the "hot" inlet of the temperator valve. Attach the tubing to the valve with a compression adapter fitting. Finally, secure the

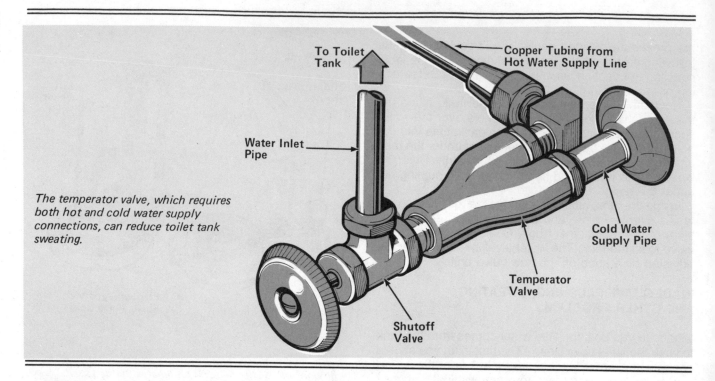

To Toilet Tank

Copper Tubing from Hot Water Supply Line

Water Inlet Pipe

The temperator valve, which requires both hot and cold water supply connections, can reduce toilet tank sweating.

Cold Water Supply Pipe

Temperator Valve

Shutoff Valve

copper tubing to the wall, and turn on the water at the main shutoff.

One of the simplest, least expensive, and most effective methods is to glue thin (¼- to ½-inch) panels of foam rubber to the inside surfaces of the tank walls. To install such panels, shut off the fixture's water supply, flush the tank, and sponge it dry. Cut pieces of foam to fit all four sides of the tank and secure them with silicone glue. Allow the glue to cure thoroughly — perhaps 24 hours — before refilling the tank.

One of the worst effects of a sweating tank is that it can hide a genuine leak in the tank. You may see water on the floor, but fail to attribute it to a leak, believing that it is merely some condensation that dripped from the tank. There is, fortunately, an easy way to check for leaks. Pour enough bluing into the tank to give the water a noticeably blue color; some toilet bowl cleaners also turn the water blue and can be used. If the tank does have a leak, the moisture on the floor will show traces of blue.

The leak may be due to loose connections or defective washers on the spud pipe or where the water inlet pipe and ballcock assembly are attached to the tank. Replace any worn gaskets or washers and tighten all of the nuts; then test with bluing in the water again. It is also possible that water is seeping out from *under* the toilet bowl. The wax ring seal that joins the bowl to the drain outlet may be defective. If this is the case, you must remove the bowl — and the tank, if it is supported by the bowl — and install a new wax gasket.

If the leak is due to a crack in the tank or bowl, you know that it is time to replace it with a new one.

Sometimes do-it-yourselfers create more problems

than they cure when they tackle toilet repairs. If you follow a few simple guidelines, you can save yourself plenty of grief — and money — when you work on the toilet. First, when you remove the tank top to see what the problem is, place the top flat on the floor well away from where you will be working. This eliminates the possibility of knocking the tank top onto the floor. Second, whenever you encounter a stubborn nut, apply some penetrating oil and do not force it with a wrench. Too much strain means a good chance for the wrench to slip off the nut and crack the tank or the bowl. Similarly, avoid overtightening tank nuts; too much pressure can also crack the toilet tank.

REMOVING AND REPLACING A TOILET

Removing and replacing a toilet is not a task to be undertaken without good reason, but it is certainly not beyond the capabilities of the well-informed do-it-yourselfer. Perhaps you have grown tired of the old fixture's appearance, or you may have cracked the bowl or the tank through the injudicious use of a wrench; or maybe you have noticed that the fixture leaks around its base. All of these situations call for the removal of the old toilet and either its reinstallation after repair or the installation of a new fixture.

Although there is nothing terribly difficult in removing and replacing a toilet, many communities prohibit — as stated in the official plumbing code — anyone but a licensed plumber from doing the job. Check the code. If it does not prohibit do-it-yourself toilet replacement — and if you feel sufficiently confident of your plumbing skill and knowledge — go ahead.

Toilet Trouble-Shooting Chart

PROBLEMS	CAUSES	REPAIRS
Water in tank runs constantly	1. Float ball or rod is misaligned.	1. Bend float rod carefully to move ball so it will not rub against side of tank.
	2. Float ball contains water.	2. Replace float ball.
	3. Float ball not rising high enough.	3. Carefully bend float rod down, but only slightly.
	4. Tank ball not seating properly at bottom of tank.	4. Remove any corrosion from lip of valve seat. Replace tank ball if worn. Adjust lift wire and guide if ball cannot seat properly.
	5. Ballcock valve does not shut off water.	5. Replace washers in ballcock assembly or, if necessary, replace entire assembly.
Toilet does not flush or flushes inadequately	1. Drain is clogged.	1. Remove blockage in drain.
	2. Not enough water in tank.	2. Raise water level in tank by bending float rod up slightly.
	3. Tank ball falls back before enough water leaves tank.	3. Move guide up so that tank ball can rise higher.
	4. Leak where tank joins toilet bowl.	4. Tighten nuts on spud pipe; replace spud washers, if necessary.
	5. Ports around underside of bowl rim clogged.	5. Ream out residue from ports.
Tank whines while filling	1. Ballcock valve not operating properly.	1. Replace washers or install new ballcock assembly.
	2. Water supply is restricted.	2. Check shutoff to see if it is completely open. Check for scale or corrosion at entry into tank and on valve.
Moisture around fixture	1. Condensation.	1. Install foam liner, tank cover, drip catcher, or temperator valve.
	2. Leak at flange wax seal.	2. Remove toilet and install new wax ring seal.
	3. Leak at bowl-tank connection.	3. Tighten spud pipe nuts; replace worn spud washers, if necessary.
	4. Leak at water inlet connection.	4. Tighten locknut and coupling nut; replace washers and gasket, if necessary.
	5. Crack in bowl or tank.	5. Replace bowl, tank, or entire fixture.

If you are installing a new toilet, the first step is to measure the rough-in distance: this is the distance from the wall behind the bowl to the center of the toilet floor drain. You can do this with the old bowl in place by measuring from the wall to the center of either of the

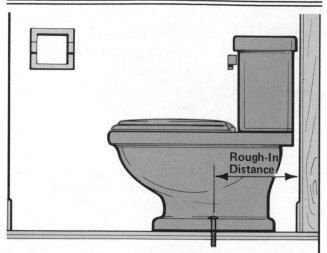

The rough-in distance can be measured with the toilet in place by measuring from the wall to the center of the hold-down bolt, or to the center of the rear bolt if the fixture is held by two pairs of bolts.

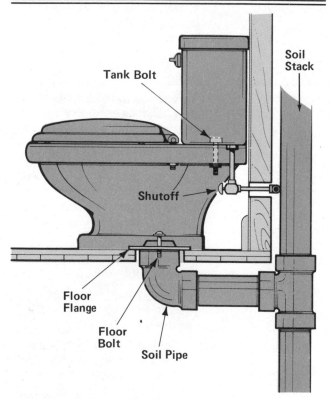

The illustration shows the typical installation of a two-piece floor-mounted toilet.

fixture's two hold-down bolts in the base. If there are four bolts, measure up to the center of the rear pair. Use this measurement when buying the new fixture so that it will fit properly in your bathroom. You can replace your old toilet with a more modern fixture, but you must make sure that your new unit will fit into the space between the outlet and the wall. You can install a smaller unit — one that will leave a space between it and the wall — but you cannot put a larger toilet into the same space that was occupied by a smaller fixture.

Once you have the new toilet, shut off the water supply to the toilet tank, and then remove all the water in both the tank and the bowl. Tripping the flush handle will eliminate most of the water from the tank, but you will need a sponge to soak up whatever water is left. Bail out the remaining water in the bowl with a small container; you will not be able to get all of it, but get as much out as you can.

If you need to remove only the bowl — leaving the tank in place — look to see whether there is a spud pipe between the bowl and the tank. It is a large pipe, found most frequently on older units, that is connected at both ends by a slip nut similar to those that hold a sink trap. The nuts that hold the spud, however, are much larger than those on a sink. You must use a spudwrench to remove the slip nuts. Once you loosen the slip nuts, slide them onto the spud itself. You should have just enough room now to remove the connecting pipe and then the bowl while the tank is still affixed to the wall.

What do you do when there is no spud pipe or when you want to remove the tank as well as the bowl? First, disconnect the water supply inlet pipe to the base of the tank. Older tanks are probably connected to the wall; newer tanks are most likely supported by the bowl. If the tank portion of your toilet is connected to the wall, remove the hanger bolts that secure the tank to the wall from inside the tank, and the pair of bolts — if present — at the bottom of the tank that connect the tank to the bowl. If the tank is supported only by the bowl, then the latter pair of bolts is all that need concern you. Remove the tank and set it out of the way. Be sure to keep the rubber gaskets you find under all the bolts; you will need them if you intend to reinstall the tank. With the tank removed from either its wall mounting or bowl support, you are ready to work on the bowl itself.

Remove the toilet seat; otherwise, it will just get in your way as you work on the bowl. Take off the caps over the hold-down bolts at the base of the bowl. You will find either two or four of these caps, most of which are made of ceramic to match the bowl. Some types are held on by plumber's joint compound and can be pried off with a putty knife; others are threaded and can be unscrewed. If you do not know which kind of caps are on your toilet, wrap the caps with masking tape to protect their finish, and try to unscrew them. If they do not come off, then you know that you must pry them off;

brush away the dried compound before proceeding.

Remove the nuts or bolts that were hidden under the caps. You may find them to be extremely stubborn, but some penetrating oil should make removal much easier. Be sure to save the washers and bolts if you will be reinstalling the bowl. Once the hold-down nuts or bolts are out, there is nothing else holding the bowl to the floor. Lift it straight up, but be sure that you have a bucket and sponge handy to take care of the water that you could not bail out earlier.

With the toilet bowl out of the way, you will find yourself looking down into an uncovered soil pipe. **Caution:** You should plug up the hole to prevent any backup of sewer gas. Tie a string around an old towel to create a good plug that you can jam into the opening, but that will not fall through into the floor drain.

Turn the bowl upside down if you are just trying to remove a clog, but be very careful when you handle either the tank or the bowl. These plumbing fixtures will crack from one sharp blow to the porcelain. Therefore, it is a good idea to have an old piece of carpet ready to serve as a work surface on which you can set the fixture.

As long as you are going to all the trouble of removing the toilet from its moorings, you might as well take the opportunity to consider any other work that might be needed to make your toilet function better than it does. For example, if the ballcock assembly has been malfunctioning, it could be a good opportunity to install a new one — especially since you have already done a great deal of the work in disconnecting the tank for removal.

Similarly, this could be a good time to install a separate water shutoff valve for the toilet if one is lacking. The fixture shutoff valve allows you to keep the water supply running everywhere else while you work on the toilet. To install the valve, follow the procedure given in "Installing a Shutoff Valve."

Putting in a new toilet and reinstalling the old one are done in the same way. Scrape away all the old putty (or other sealing material) from both the bottom of the bowl and the metal or plastic floor flange with a putty knife. Inspect the flange and the bolts that come up from the flange. If anything is amiss — the flange damaged or the bolts stripped — replace the part or parts before you go any further. All of these parts are inexpensive, and it is far better to replace them than to try to get by with parts of doubtful quality.

The next step is to put a new sealer ring on the water outlet opening on the bottom of the new bowl; the best and easiest type to install is the wax toilet bowl gasket. Put the wax ring in place on the bottom of the bowl while the fixture is upside down. (If your floor flange is recessed, you will need a gasket with a plastic sleeve in the wax; this sleeve faces toward you as you position it since it will go into the soil pipe.) Now, apply a uniform layer of toilet-bowl setting compound — about ⅛ inch

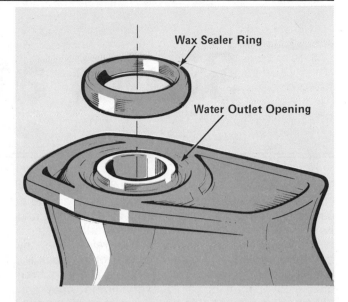

The wax sealer ring, or gasket, is put in place while the fixture is upside down. If the floor flange is recessed, you will need a gasket with a plastic sleeve in the wax.

thick — around the edge of the bowl at the base. You can buy the compound — sort of a caulking — at most hardware stores and at all plumbing supply dealers.

Turn the bowl right-side-up and place it down over the flange, guiding the bolts in place. Press down firmly, and give the bowl a slight twist to make certain that the wax ring seats properly against the flange. It is, of course, of utmost importance that the bowl be level; check this by placing a level across the bowl. Either press down on any higher portion or insert thin wedges (you can hide them with toilet bowl setting compound) under any lower portion of the bowl to even it. Whatever you do, however, make sure that you do nothing that would disturb or break the seal of the wax ring.

Once you get the bowl positioned properly, you can install the nuts to hold the bowl to the floor. Remember: Do not overtighten the nuts. If you do, you can crack the fixture, and hand-tightening is all that is required anyway. Coat the hold-down nuts and bolts with toilet bowl setting compound and reinstall the caps.

That completes the installation of the bowl; now you are ready to attach the tank. Rebolt a wall-mounted tank, or reinstall the bolts and washers that connect a bowl-supported tank. Naturally, before you put them back, make sure that all the washers, gaskets, and bolts are still in sound condition. If the tank and bowl are connected with a spud pipe, apply pipe joint compound to the threads of the spud slip nuts and tighten them in place. Finally, reconnect the water supply inlet pipe to the tank, making sure the ballcock assembly is properly attached, and turn the water back on.

Sinks and Tubs

Many people who rush to call a plumber when a pipe springs a leak or a toilet gets clogged, draw the line at calling in professional help when it comes to sinks and tubs. They feel that it takes no great expertise to stop a faucet from dripping or to clear a slow drain — and they are right. Hopefully, the other sections of this book will encourage you to tackle pipe problems and toilet troubles as well, but certainly every homeowner and apartment-dweller should be able to maintain and repair most sink and tub problems without paying for a plumber.

TOOLS FOR SINKS AND TUBS

Most likely, you already possess a great many of the necessary tools for working on sinks and tubs. For the most part, they are tools that can be used for many other do-it-yourself projects besides plumbing chores, or they are tools that are so well-known that no detailed explanation of them is required here. For example, a must for every household is the plumber's friend — also called a plunger or a force pump. The best models have long handles, and their suction cups are large enough to cover different types of drain openings.

Plumber's snakes or drain-and-trap augers come in various lengths; you should have both a short and a long one. If you plan to buy an auger, look for one that comes encased in a metal housing — it is far less messy to use. A plumber's tape or ribbon looks like a long clock spring.

You will need wrenches for most faucet repairs and for various other connections. A medium-size adjustable wrench is a fine tool to have, because it can be used on nuts of many different sizes; with one adjust-

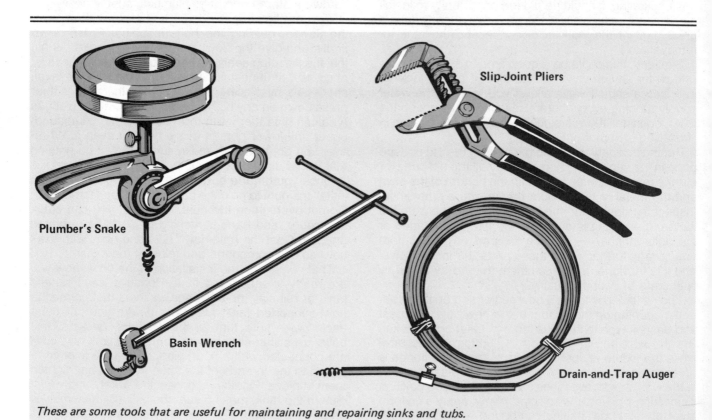

These are some tools that are useful for maintaining and repairing sinks and tubs.

Plumber's Snake

Basin Wrench

Slip-Joint Pliers

Drain-and-Trap Auger

able wrench you can handle the same tasks that would otherwise necessitate a complete set of open-end wrenches. Open-end wrenches, however, do have an advantage over an adjustable wrench because they provide a secure grip on the nut. Of course, you can frequently substitute a pair of long handled, slip-joint pliers for either kind of wrench.

A basin wrench is a specialized tool that allows you to reach tight spots under sinks and basins. The jaws of a basin wrench not only adjust to accommodate nuts of different sizes, but they also flip over to the opposite side, so that you can keep turning without first removing the wrench. If you plan to work on tub and shower fixtures, then there is a good chance that you will need a socket wrench set to remove recessed packing nuts. If you do not already own a socket wrench set, it may not pay to buy one just for this job; but you can find many uses for a socket wrench set besides do-it-yourself plumbing chores.

ELIMINATING FAUCET DRIPS

Although a dripping faucet is the most common plumbing problem — and one of the easiest to repair — many people try to ignore it, and they leave the dripping faucet unrepaired. They think, apparently, that a tiny drip is not worth the effort to fix, but those people would be amazed to learn how much that tiny drip costs. A steady drip can add up to so many gallons over a year's time that it can end up costing about $50 in wasted water. Multiply that figure by the number of faucet drips in your home, and you can calculate how much of your money is literally going down the drain. If that is not enough to convince you, just think about the drip that comes from a hot water faucet; in that case, you are also paying to heat water before you waste it.

A drip is caused by seepage. Remember that the fresh water supply enters your house or apartment under pressure. Therefore, there must be a watertight seal holding back the incoming water when the faucet handle is in the "off" position. That seal is usually created by a washer pressed tightly against the faucet seat. Obviously when the washer or the seat is not functioning properly, a little water can seep through and drip out of the faucet spout. To stop the drip, all you usually do is replace the washer or repair the seat.

Naturally, the first thing to do when fixing a faucet drip is to turn off the water supply. You should be able to turn off the supply at a nearby shutoff; but if your house is not equipped with shutoffs for individual fixtures, then you must go to the main shutoff and stop the entire water supply throughout your home.

The Typical Compression-Type Faucet

With the water flow stopped, you can start to disassemble the faucet. No matter what the faucet looks like,

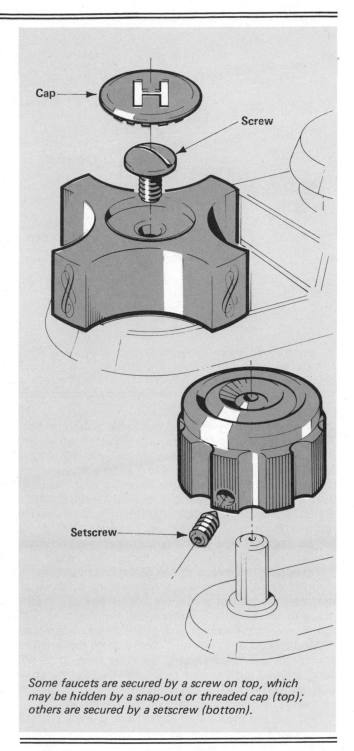

Some faucets are secured by a screw on top, which may be hidden by a snap-out or threaded cap (top); others are secured by a setscrew (bottom).

whether it has separate handles for hot and cold water, or just one that operates hot and cold water, it operates according to certain basic principles. The first thing to do is to remove the faucet handle, which is held to the main body of the faucet by a tiny screw — either on the top or at the back of the handle. You may not be able to see a top-mounted screw at first, because some of

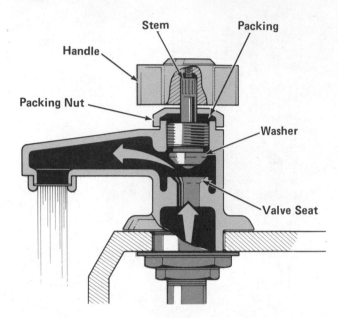

Stem   Packing

Handle

Packing Nut

Washer

Valve Seat

A typical compression-type stem faucet is shown in cross-section.

them are hidden by a metal or plastic button or disc. These buttons usually snap out, although some are threaded. Once you get the button out, you will see the top-mounted handle screw. If a handle's screw — no matter where it is located — is exceptionally difficult to turn, use a little penetrating oil to help loosen it. Often, a standard blade or Phillips screwdriver can be used to remove the screw. Sometimes, however, the handle will be secured by a setscrew; an Allen wrench (hexkey wrench) will be required to loosen this type.

Take the handle off and look at the faucet assembly. You will see a packing nut (sometimes called the bonnet); remove the nut with either a large pair of slip-joint pliers or an adjustable wrench, but take special care not to scar the metal. It is a good idea to wrap tape around the packing nut to protect it from the teeth of your pliers or wrench. Once you get the packing nut off, you can twist out the stem (sometimes called the spindle) by turning it in the same direction (counterclockwise) you would to turn on the faucet.

You can see the washer at the base of the stem, but to remove it you must first take out the brass screw that holds it. That can be difficult, but some penetrating oil should make a stubborn brass screw much easier to remove. After you remove the screw, examine it to see whether it needs replacement along with the washer. If you cannot get the brass screw out, do not despair; you can buy a whole new stem, if necessary.

Look for the size on the old washer. It is absolutely essential that you put on a replacement washer that is *exactly* the right size. Washers that "almost fit" will

"almost stop the drip." Also note whether the old washer is beveled or flat; the shape is important too. If you cannot determine the precise size, take the whole stem with you to the hardware store. You also can buy a big assortment pack of washers that contains just about every size and shape you might need.

Some washers, however, do not work well on a hot water faucet. A washer designed only for cold water expands greatly when it gets hot, thereby closing the opening and slowing the flow of hot water. Perhaps you have experienced a hot water faucet that works fine until the water gets quite hot; then it slows to a trickle. Be sure to tell your hardware dealer whether the replacement washer you need is for the hot side or the cold side. Some washers will work for either. You also can obtain a swivel-head washer with a fitting that snaps into the threaded screw hole in the base of the stem.

Fasten the new washer to the stem, and reinstall the assembly in the faucet. Turn the stem the same direction that you would turn the faucet handle to stop the water flow (clockwise). With the stem in place, put the packing nut back on, but be careful not to scar the metal with the wrench. Once you screw on the handle and replace the button or disc, your faucet is completely reassembled. Turn the water supply back on, and you should find that your days of wasting water (and money!) are over.

Other Types of Faucets

Instead of washers, some faucets use rubber diaphragms to control the flow of water. If you have this type of faucet, you may have to remove the faucet stem from the faucet body with a pair of pliers. Be sure to wrap the top of the stem with tape to protect it from the teeth of the pliers. The rubber diaphragm covers the bottom of the stem, and you may have to pry it off with a screwdriver. Make sure the replacement diaphragm fits over the base of the stem snugly before reassembling the faucet.

Another type of faucet uses a rubber seat ring that acts like a washer. To remove it from the stem, you will have to use pliers to hold the end of the faucet stem while you unscrew the threaded centerpiece that holds the seat ring in place. Remove the sleeve to insert the new seat ring, but be sure that the seat ring's lettering faces the threaded part of the stem.

Cartridge-type stem faucets may have a spring and a rubber washer. To replace these, lift the cartridge out of the faucet body and remove the washer and spring from the faucet body. Simply insert the new spring and washer in place, and carefully align the cartridge so it fits correctly into the slots in the faucet body when reassembling it.

There also are faucets with washers that have the faucet seat built into the stem itself. This type of assembly lifts from the base in a removable sleeve, which contains the valve seat. Unscrew the stem nut from the base of the stem and remove the metal washer and washer retainer that contains a rubber washer. The new washer can be inserted — bevel-side-up — into the washer retainer.

One type of faucet does not have washers at all; it works by means of two metal discs. Turning the faucet on aligns holes in the discs and allows water to flow through the faucet. If something malfunctions with this type of faucet, the valve assembly is usually replaced.

Repairing a Faucet Valve Seat

Sometimes a faucet may still drip after you have replaced a washer. This indicates that there may be something wrong with the faucet valve seat. Perhaps a defective washer at some point in the past allowed the metal stem to grind against the seat and leave it uneven, or else chemicals in the water have built up a residue that now prevents the washer from fitting tightly against the valve seat.

What do you do to repair a bad faucet seat? You can use a valve seat grinder, or dresser. This is an inexpensive tool that will even out a worn seat, but you must be careful not to use the tool too long or with too much force because the seat is made of soft metal and you can grind too much of it away quite easily. To use this tool, you remove the faucet stem and insert the seat grinder down to the valve seat in the faucet body. Using moderate pressure, turn the tool clockwise a few times. Then, clean the valve seat with a cloth to remove any metal shavings. The other thing you can do is to replace the seat — a necessity if you grind it down too far with the tool. Removal of the old valve seat is fairly

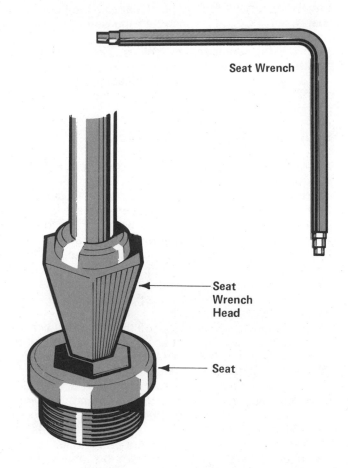

Seat Wrench

Seat Wrench Head

Seat

If a faucet's valve seat is worn too much and cannot be evened out with a seat grinder, it can usually be removed with a seat wrench.

Shown are two types of seat grinders, or dressers, for evening out a worn seat valve.

simple if you have the right tool, called a seat wrench. Just insert the seat wrench into the seat and turn it counterclockwise. Once you get the old seat out, be sure that the replacement seat you buy is an exact duplicate. On occasion, you may have a valve seat that is impossible to remove; in such a case, you can insert a seat sleeve that slides into place in the old seat and provides a tight seal.

STOPPING FAUCET LEAKS

A drip occurs when the faucet is turned off; a faucet leak occurs with the water running. If you see water coming out around the handle, you have a faucet leak.

The first thing to do is to make sure that the faucet's packing nut is tight (but be careful not to scratch the nut with pliers or a wrench). If you find a loose nut is not causing the leak, you should then replace the packing. Faucet packing can be a solid piece of packing; it can consist of one or more rubber O-rings; or it can resemble string or soft wire that is wrapped around the stem under the packing nut.

To replace the packing, shut off the water supply and remove the faucet handle. Loosen the packing nut and slip both the nut and the old packing up off the stem. Put the new packing on. If you use the string-like packing material, wrap a few turns around the stem; packing that resembles soft wire is wrapped around the stem only once. Before you finish reassembling the faucet, smear a light coat of petroleum jelly on the threads of the stem and on the threads of the packing nut.

Kitchen faucets — the kind where the spout swings from side to side — present a somewhat different situation. These faucets contain one or more O-rings to prevent water from oozing out around the spout. If the ring wears out, you will see water at the base of the spout every time you turn on the water. To replace an O-ring,

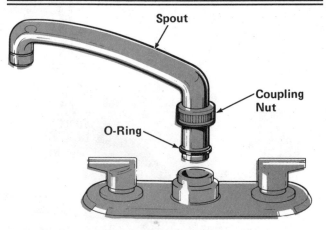

Some kitchen faucets contain one or more O-rings to prevent water from oozing out around the spout. Worn O-rings can be easily replaced.

shut off the water supply and remove the threaded coupling nut that holds the spout in place by turning it counterclockwise. Be sure to wrap the nut with tape to prevent scratching it with pliers or a wrench. With the coupling nut removed you can work the spout up and out of its socket, where you will find the ring(s). Replace the defective ring(s). Be sure to use exactly the same size, and reassemble the faucet.

Single-lever faucets are simple to fix as well, but there are so many different types that you must purchase a specific repair kit for the faucet you have. Generally, a faucet company makes repair kits for its products and includes detailed instructions and diagrams with the replacement parts. The hardest part of repairing a single-lever faucet may be in tracking down the hardware dealer or plumbing supply store that carries the appropriate kit. Once you have the kit, however, you should find little difficulty in eliminating the leak. Just make sure that the water supply is shut off before disassembling a single-lever faucet, and follow the kit directions carefully.

SILENCING NOISY FAUCETS

Faucets can scream, whistle or chatter when you turn them on or off. There are several possible causes for these ear-shattering phenomena. If your house is newly constructed, you may have pipes that are too small to allow the water to pass through them properly. Similarly, pipes in older homes can become restricted by the formation of scale, with the same result — a noisy faucet. In either case, you must replace the pipes to get rid of the noise.

Most likely, however, your noisy faucet is caused by a washer that is either of the wrong size or is not being held securely to the stem. Turn off the water supply before starting this or any other faucet repair job. Just replace the washer, or tighten it, and you should eliminate the noise. If the faucet still makes noise, check the washer seat; the seat can get partially closed with residue, and the restricted water flow then can whistle or chatter. If this is the case, clean the seat.

A terrible squealing noise when you turn the faucet handle means the metal threads of the stem are binding against the faucet's threads. Remove the stem and coat both sets of threads with petroleum jelly. The lubrication should stop the noise and make the handle easier to turn. Of course, if the stem threads or faucet body threads have become worn, the resulting play between them causes vibration and noise in the faucet. You will need more than just lubrication to quiet such a faucet. Install a new stem and see if the noise vanishes. If not, it means that the faucet body threads are worn, and the only solution is a completely new faucet. Fortunately, the stem is the part that usually wears first; but even if you must replace the entire faucet, you will find it to be an easy do-it-yourself project.

REPLACING A FAUCET

Replacing a faucet — for either functional or aesthetic reasons — gets you into a little more work than just changing a washer or putting in a new faucet valve seat. Fortunately, new faucet units are made for do-it-yourself installation, with easy-to-follow instructions included. A new faucet can work wonders for the appearance of your old fixtures, and — even better — it will eliminate all the leaks, drips, and other problems you may have had with your former faucet.

Suppose, for example, that you want to replace the old faucet on your kitchen sink with a modern single-handle unit. Just make sure that whatever unit you select, it will cover the old faucet's mounting holes. Generally that is no great problem; but some sinks — especially older ones — can be somewhat unusual. If you have an unusual sink, look for an adjustable faucet unit that is made to fit many types of sinks. Once you select the faucet model that you want, follow this general procedure to install it properly:

Cut off both hot and cold water supplies to the sink faucets. Disconnect the old faucets from their water supply lines under the sink. The connections will probably be threaded compression fittings that are held by locknuts. Loosen the nuts with an adjustable wrench or basin wrench, and disconnect the water supply pipes from the faucets.

The old faucets are probably held in place by nuts underneath the sink. Loosen and remove these nuts. (In most cases, these nuts are almost impossible to remove without loosening them with a basin wrench.)

If the old assembly has a spray head and hose, remove the spray head mounting nut under the sink; also disconnect the hose from its spout connection. Now you should be able to completely remove the old faucet assembly from the sink. Clean the sink around the faucet mounting area.

Before you install the new faucet unit, apply plumber's putty around its base. (If gaskets are supplied with the faucet for this purpose, you need not use putty.) Then, insert the new faucet assembly in place on the sink.

NOTE: If the sink has a spray hose, it generally is a good idea to attach it first, if possible. Run the spray hose down through its opening in the faucet assembly, through its opening in the sink, and up through the sink's center opening. Attach the hose to the supply stub on the faucet.

With the new faucet assembly in position, place the washers and nuts on the assembly's mounting studs under the sink, and hand-tighten them, making sure that the assembly is in proper position and any gaskets are correctly aligned. Then tighten the nuts with a basin wrench.

Align the original water supply lines with the flexible supply tubes coming from the new faucet and connect

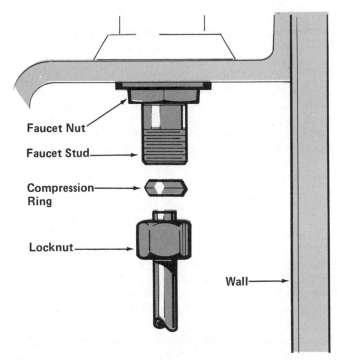

The faucet is secured to the sink by a nut under the basin. The water supply line is usually connected to the faucet with a threaded compression fitting.

them with compression couplings. Make sure that the hot and cold water lines are connected to the proper supply tubes on the faucet assembly. When you attach the lines, be sure to use two wrenches — one to hold the fitting, the other to turn the nut on the water supply line. NOTE: If the combined length of the old supply line and new supply tubes is inconveniently long, you can cut off a portion of the original lines before attaching the coupling. Conversely, if the new supply tubes reach all the way to shutoff valves under the sink, the tubes can be connected directly to the valves with a compression fitting. Also, on some installations, you may need adapters or transition fittings to join different size supply lines and tubes or to connect one type of pipe to another.

Now, turn on the hot and cold water supplies to the fixture, and run both hot and cold water full force to clear the supply lines and to check the fixture for leaks. If there is evidence of leakage, go back over the procedure to check for loose or improper connections.

A bathroom lavatory faucet can be replaced using essentially the same procedures. One difference may be the presence of a pop-up drain that is connected by a linkage to a knob or plunger on the old faucet assembly. There should be one or two places in the linkage where it can be easily disconnected from the faucet before removing the original unit from the basin. (See the section entitled "Lavatory and Tub Stoppers" later in this chapter for more detailed information.) Be sure to reconnect the drain linkage when installing the new faucet.

Shower and tub faucets, meanwhile, can be a bit more complicated since the connections are not made under a sink but rather behind a wall. Whoever built your home should have provided an access panel to allow you to get at the pipes without ripping the wall apart. If you find that you must cut into the wall, however, be sure to add an access panel for pipe and faucet repairs.

Actually, once you get to the tub faucet connections behind the wall, the job is no harder than working on your kitchen sink. Just shut off the water supply, remove the faucet handle on the tub side, and then disconnect the old faucet unit from the back. If present, unscrew the old shower head pipe from its pipe inside the wall; do the same thing with the tub spout. Now you are ready to install all the new parts. Just follow the directions that are included with the new assembly.

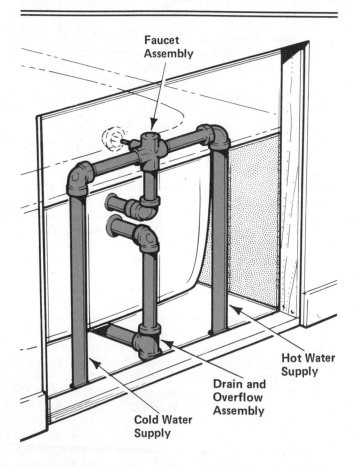

Replacing tub faucets can be a bit complicated because the connections are behind a wall. There should, however, be an access panel so you can reach the connections.

AERATORS

A standard kitchen sink spout can deliver a great quantity of water in a hurry, especially if the water pressure happens to be high. If it is not carefully controlled, a lot of splashing and splattering is the usual result. This problem can be overcome simply by the installation of an aerator, a small device that draws in and mixes air with the water stream. The resulting flow from the spout is even, quiet and splashless, and the water tends to cling to and flow evenly across objects in the sink. There are many different models of aerators available, all inexpensive, and you can easily install one on your own kitchen sink spout.

Though there are many variations, an aerator consists basically of a spout adapter and washer seals, a perforated disc, one or more screens, an outer body with air-intake slots, and perhaps an inner body as well. The simplest type terminates in a flexible rubber sleeve that slips over the end of the spout; though easy to install, this type is also prone to pop off unexpectedly. Other types either screw onto or into spouts that are already threaded. Some aerators are held in place by internal-expanding adapters set inside the end of the spout. To fit an aerator of this type, take careful measurements of your faucet spout and choose a unit that is either an exact or extremely close fit.

Aerators must be cleaned periodically, because their screens become clogged with tiny bits of sediment, grit or scale, and mineral deposits sometimes build up around the air slots. If you note that the water stream is uneven or the aeration level has diminished, or if water begins to squirt out of the air intake slots, it is time to clean the aerator. Remove it by hand. (However, if you must use pliers, wrap tape around the aerator to keep from scratching it.) Disassemble the unit — usually by unscrewing it — and backflush the screens and the disc inside it with a strong stream of water. Be careful the parts do not get washed down the drain! Dry the parts, and brush them gently with a fine-bristled — but fairly stiff — brush. Mineral deposits can sometimes be removed by soaking the parts in vinegar, or you may be able to scrape them away gently with a penknife. Reassemble the aerator, making sure that you get all of the parts positioned in the proper order and direction.

REPAIRING A SPRAY HEAD

Many modern sink faucet assemblies are fitted with spray head units that occasionally leak or malfunction. The assembly consists of a special diverter valve assembly located within the spout body, a flexible hose connected to the spout beneath the sink, and a spray head with an activating lever and an aerator assembly. The spray head body and lever is generally a sealed unit, and if it malfunctions or fails, the unit must be replaced with another identical unit. Other parts of the spray system, however, can be repaired.

The aerator portion of the spray head is similar to a sink spout aerator, through the parts are usually held together with a small retaining screw. If aeration is inadequate or water squirts off at various angles, cleaning is required and can be performed in about the same way as in a spout aerator. Water dripping off the flexible hose beneath the sink indicates a leak at the hose-to-spout connection, the hose-to-spray head connection, or somewhere in the hose itself. Dry the hose thoroughly with a paper towel and check the head connection; this may or may not be repairable. If the leak is at this point, tighten the connection, disassemble and make repairs, or replace the head and hose assembly. Next, check the spout connection under the sink. Tightening may stop a leak here; otherwise, disconnect the hose, apply plumber's joint compound or wrap plumber's joint tape around the threads, and reconnect it. The easiest way to spot a leak in the hose is to inspect it inch by inch under a strong light while water is running through the hose. Look particularly for tiny cracks, chafes or indications of some mechanical damage. Temporary repairs can be made by wrapping a slightly damaged section of hose with vinyl electrical tape; but replacement of the hose will eventually be necessary.

Uneven water flow, low pressure when the pressure at other faucets seems all right, or troublesome switching back and forth from spray head to sink spout can be caused by a malfunctioning diverter valve or by a restricted hose. To check the hose, remove the spray head at the coupling — if possible — and disconnect the coupling from the hose by prying off the snap-ring retainer. Turn on the water and allow a forceful stream of water to flow into the hose. If a strong stream of water flows out of the open end of the hose, then you know the diverter valve is the source of the trouble. A weak stream flowing from the open end of the hose may indicate a blockage in the hose itself. Running the water full-force for a brief time may clear the hose. If not, remove the hose from the spout attachment, stretch it out straight, and sight through it toward a strong light source. If the hose appears to be clear, the problem lies in the diverter valve. If not, you may be able to clear the obstruction with a wire coat hanger or a length of wire. Failing that, replace the hose; if you cannot obtain an exact replacement, adapters are available for connecting other types and sizes.

To service the diverter valve, you must first remove the sink spout: loosen the screw on top, unscrew the threaded spout ring or nut, and lift the spout out of its socket. This exposes the valve; some are just set in place and can be lifted straight out by gripping them with a pair of pliers, while others are secured by a screw. If there is a screw, turn it enough to free the valve. If possible, disassemble the valve. Flush all the parts with water and clean all the surfaces and aper-

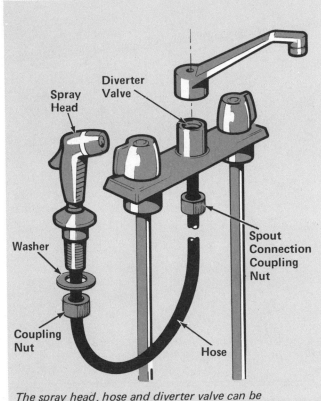

The spray head, hose and diverter valve can be disconnected and removed for repair or replacement.

tures with a toothpick (never use metal instruments). Reassemble and reinstall the valve, and test the unit. If it still operates poorly, you will probably have to replace the valve. The replacement must be exact, so take the faucet manufacturer's name and the unit model number, or the old valve, along when you purchase a new valve.

ADDING A WATER OUTLET

What about those situations in which you would like to have a faucet where none exists now? For example, you may want to add a drinking fountain to the middle of an exposed cold water pipe that runs up an exterior wall, or you may like to have a faucet near your new built-in bar. You probably think that putting in either of these new additions would require a great deal of plumbing expertise — cutting into the pipe and installing special fittings — but you can do these things yourself more easily than you ever thought possible.

There is a secret to adding a water faucet to copper or galvanized steel pipe without having to cut, thread or solder pipe; the secret is a fitting called the saddle tee, which is composed of a clamp that fits around the back of the water supply pipe and bolts to a front fitting that has a threaded opening to accommodate a faucet. The

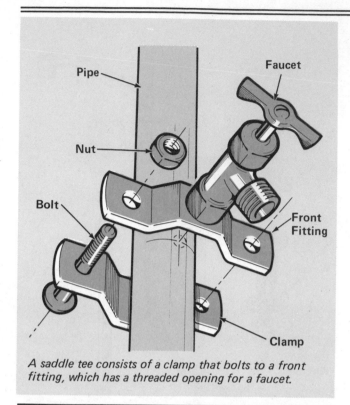

Pipe

Faucet

Nut

Bolt

Front Fitting

Clamp

A saddle tee consists of a clamp that bolts to a front fitting, which has a threaded opening for a faucet.

threaded openings come in several sizes for various popular connections, and the device is made to fit several pipe sizes. The front fitting may be backed by a washer or gasket; and the fitting has a hole through which the water flows from the pipe.

Installation is simple. Place the saddle tee on the water supply pipe at the point where you would like to have the water outlet. Attach the tee and clamp with the nuts. Tighten the nuts to hold the two pieces together securely. Turn off the water supply to that pipe. Drill a hole straight through the front fitting's opening into the *front wall* of the water pipe. A hand drill is the best tool to use for this purpose, even though it is somewhat slow. A power drill is much faster, but it could go through both the front and the back of the pipe before you can stop it. Therefore, use a hand drill with a bit that will make a hole in the pipe as large as the hole in the front fitting. After you drill the hole, there will be metal shavings in the threaded opening. Remove the shavings by blowing them out with a squeeze bottle; never try to blow the chips out with your breath because you could blow them right into your eyes.

The only thing remaining to be done is the installation of the faucet itself. Apply plumber's joint compound or tape to the threads and screw the faucet into the threaded connector of the saddle tee. That is all there is to it; just turn on the water supply, and you have an outlet exactly where you want one.

Saddle tees are extremely versatile plumbing devices. You can purchase them for copper or galvanized steel pipes and for either hot or cold water. You can put in a saddle tee when you want to connect a branch pipe to a main pipe or to make any other threaded connection to a fixture. For example, you can hook up a dishwasher or a clothes washer with a saddle tee. For the latter, you would need to tap into both hot and cold water pipes; in this case, you would just install a faucet on each supply pipe and connect hoses to carry water to the appliance.

One of the best saddle tee installations — best because a professional will probably charge you $25 or more for doing the same work — is the one that connects the water supply to the ice-making device in your new refrigerator. In fact, for a few dollars you can buy a kit that contains both the saddle tee and the connector for the copper tubing.

INSTALLING A SHUTOFF VALVE

Any plumber who installs a fixture without also installing a shutoff, or supply stop valve, is only doing a partial job. You will discover the truth of this statement — if you have not already — the next time a plumbing crisis occurs and you must waste precious time running to the main water shutoff valve.

Fortunately, you can add shutoffs to your plumbing fixtures at relatively modest cost. Whether you work on a sink, basin, appliance or toilet tank, the shutoff principle is the same. You must remove a section of water supply pipe that runs to the fixture from the floor or the wall, attach the shutoff valve to the remaining piece of pipe sticking out of the floor or wall (called the stubout), and then connect the shutoff to the fixture with a flexible pipe, usually a chrome-plated copper tube.

The kind of stub-out pipe you have dictates the kind of fittings that you will need. A threaded pipe naturally requires a threaded shutoff; a copper stub-out takes an adapter that you must sweat-solder at one end, but which is threaded at the other end to accept a threaded shutoff valve. For flexible copper tubing and some plastic pipe, mechanical adapters can be obtained. Rigid plastic pipe, however, requires a plastic adapter that is screwed to the shutoff valve and solvent-welded to the plastic stub-out. If the stub-out comes from the wall and the fixture is located above it, for example, you need an angled stop valve to turn the water flow at a right angle. However, if the stub-out for that fixture comes from the floor, you use a straight stop valve.

The flexible chrome-plated copper tube, or connector, makes installing the final connections easy, because it save you from cutting or piecing pipe together to join the shutoff valve to the fixture. The connectors come in different styles for different purposes: one with a flat head or flange is for a toilet tank connection; one with a bayonet head is for a lavatory; and one with a threaded tip is for a kitchen sink. The connector is joined to the shutoff valve by a flare connection, compression fitting or compression ring fitting.

To install a shutoff valve on, for example, a lavatory that has galvanized steel supply pipes which run from the wall to an overhead faucet, follow this basic procedure: Turn off the water supply at the main shutoff. Then disconnect the water supply pipe at the lavatory faucet by loosening the coupling nut under the faucet with a basin wrench; the loosened nut should slide down the upper portion of pipe (sometimes called the tailpiece). It may be possible to free the tailpiece by carefully pulling it down and moving it to one side. However, it often is easiest to simply cut a small section out of the water supply pipe with a hacksaw just above the elbow fitting fastened to the wall stub-out. If there is not enough room to cut the pipe, you may have to loosen the faucet itself.

Once the supply pipe above the elbow fitting has been cut through and both pieces have been removed, apply one pipe wrench to the stub-out, and another pipe wrench to the elbow fitting. Unscrew the elbow fitting while holding the stub-out with one wrench to keep it from turning. NOTE: If the joints are sweat-soldered to copper pipe, they will have to be melted. Follow the procedures outlined in the section "Sweat-Soldering" earlier in the book. Rigid plastic pipe can be cut with a hacksaw.

Apply plumber's joint compound or tape to the threads on the pipe stub coming out of the wall. Screw on an angled shutoff valve, tightening it with an adjustable wrench while the stub-out is kept from turning with a pipe wrench. Connect a flexible chrome-plated copper tube, or connector, of suitable length with coupling nuts at each end. The end that will connect to the faucet should have a bayonet head; the end that will connect to the shut-off valve should have a compression ring. Connect the flexible tube to the shutoff valve, tightening it with an adjustable wrench. Connect the other end to the faucet, using a basin wrench.

Repeat the procedure for the other faucet, and turn the water supply back on. Run the water full force to clear the lines, and check all connections and joints for leaks.

TRAP REPLACEMENT

Directly beneath the drain outlet of your kitchen sink, and every bathroom lavatory, is the trap. This element is vital not only to the proper functioning of the drainage system, but to your health and safety as well. Each trap contains, and maintains, a "plug" of water within its curved section that acts as a seal against the entrance of harmful sewer gases. If the trap leaks, this water barrier may disappear and create a hazardous situation. All traps must be kept in proper working order and good condition. Restrictions and clogging are immediately noticeable because the drainage flow is slowed or stopped; clearing the blockage takes care of

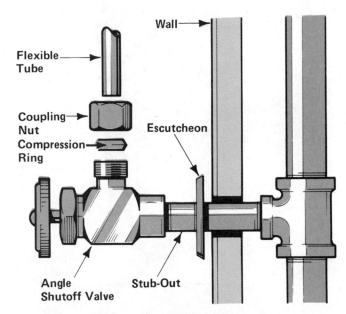

The shutoff valve is connected to the stub-out. A flexible water supply tube runs from the valve to the faucet.

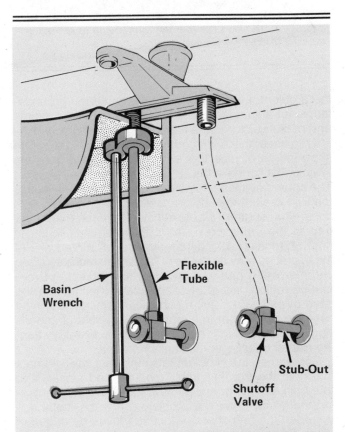

Because there is very little room under the lavatory, you will probably need a basin wrench to tighten the coupling nuts.

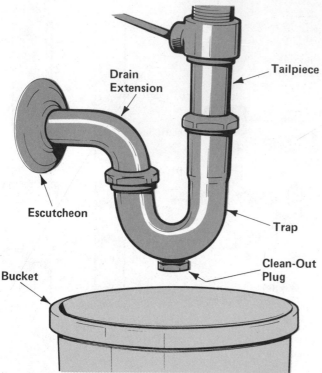

Some sink or lavatory traps have a clean-out plug that enables you to clean the trap without having to remove it from the drain.

the problem. Leakage or seepage can often go undetected for a time, so check your traps from time to time and make quick repairs if anything seems amiss.

Trap assemblies are comprised of several parts. The short length of pipe that extends downward from the drain outlet flange in the sink or lavatory is the tailpiece. The curved section of pipe connected to the tailpiece is the trap itself. It may be one piece or two coupled sections. The length of pipe extending from the end of the trap to the drainpipe outlet in the wall or floor is the drain extension. It may be straight or curved. All of these pieces may be made of rather thin metal — often chrome-plated brass — and they are subject to eventual corrosion, failure of seals, and sometimes, in the case of exposed traps, mechanical damage. Damage can also result from frequent reaming with a plumber's auger. Whatever the reasons for failure, a malfunctioning trap should be immediately repaired.

Sometimes the problem is simply that the slip nuts that hold the trap assembly together and secure it to the drain and the drainpipe have loosened; just tightening them may solve the problem. But if the metal has corroded through, the slip-nut threads are damaged or other damage has occurred, the only solution is replacement. Trap assemblies and parts to fit just about any possible installation requirement are readily avail-

able at most hardware and all plumbing supply stores. Chrome-plated thin-wall brass traps are popular, especially where appearance is important. Polypropylene (PP) plastic traps feature ruggedness and longevity, and will outperform all other types. ABS plastic traps are also in use, but are susceptible to deformation and eventual failure when handling frequent passage of boiling water and caustic household chemicals. And, they may not be allowed by your local plumbing code. Irrespective of the material, you are likely to encounter two trap diameters — 1½-inch traps for kitchen sinks, and 1¼-inch traps for lavatories.

Trap replacement is simple in most cases. If the trap is equipped with a clean-out plug on the bottom of the curved section, remove the plug with a wrench and allow the water in the trap to drain into a bucket. Otherwise, unscrew the slip nuts and slide them out of the way. If the trap is a swivel type, the curved trap section(s) will come free. However, keep the trap upright as you remove it and pour the water out after the part is free. If it is a fixed trap that does not swivel, remove the tailpiece slip nut at the drain flange and the slip nut at the top of the trap, and shove the tailpiece down into the trap itself. Then twist the trap clockwise until you can drain the water in the trap, pull the tailpiece free, and unscrew the trap from the drain extension or drainpipe.

Installation of a new trap is merely a reverse procedure of the disassembly. Purchase a trap of the proper diameter, or a universal type that will work on either size drain, as well as a new tailpiece, drain extension or other fittings as necessary. A swivel trap is the easiest to work with, because it can be easily adjusted for angled or misaligned drainpipe/fixture installations. A clean-out plug on a trap is handy but not essential, because the trap can be taken apart for cleaning if necessary. Replace the new parts in appropriate order, making sure that you have the slip nuts and compression seals, or large washers, lined up on the proper pipe sections. Couple the parts together loosely with the slip nuts, make the final adjustments for correct pipe alignment, and tighten the nuts down snug, but not too tight. Plumber's joint compound or tape is not usually necessary, but you can use either if you prefer. Run water into the new trap immediately, both to check for leaks and to fill the trap with water to provide that important barrier against sewer gases.

MODERNIZING LAVATORIES AND TUBS

There is no reason why you have to live with plumbing fixtures that are either inefficient or unattractive, or both. Do you have a bathtub that is perched up so high on legs that you feel as though you must pole vault to get into it? Or perhaps the surface of your lavatory basin is severely stained and nicked. There may even be places in your home where you want to add new plumbing facilities in areas that had none before: a half bath in the basement or a guest powder room in what is now a large closet. All of these additions make your home more convenient and, of course, more valuable.

The best part, naturally, is that you can install many of the plumbing fixtures yourself, thereby saving a great deal of money. Since the idea is to improve your home, however, install the best fixtures you can afford.

Remodeling or modernizing — in contrast to many other plumbing projects — allows you to take your time and plan everything carefully. Most likely, you have lived with the old fixtures for some time, and a few more weeks will not make any difference. This is no emergency situation that demands a quick decision. Take your time and investigate all the new types of fixtures that can enhance the efficiency as well as the appearance of your home.

There is one other thing that you must investigate before you start replacing old fixtures or adding new ones: the local plumbing code. Almost every community has a plumbing code that governs the materials and procedures required for all plumbing work, and some codes specify that only a licensed plumber can perform certain plumbing installations. Such a provision may compel you to contract with a plumber for part of the job while doing the rest yourself. In any case, familiarize yourself thoroughly with all the code's provisions, and do only the work which you are legally allowed to do.

Usually, the building inspector's office in your city has copies of the code. If there is no such office, check city, county or state offices until you find the code. Check with the same people about obtaining a plumbing permit. The authority will check your plumbing project to insure that your plans meet the requirements of the code, and an inspector will inspect it afterwards to see that the work was done properly. Plumbing must be done right; otherwise, the health of your family and the well-being of your entire neighborhood could be endangered.

Removing and installing a lavatory is easily a one-person job, although an assistant often can be helpful for lifting and balancing a cumbersome unit. A fiberglass bathtub also can be handled by one person, if necessary. However, a steel tub can weigh more than 250 pounds and requires at least two people to handle. A cast-iron tub will weigh even more, and it will take at least three people to maneuver it.

Before disconnecting any fixture, you must turn off the water supply. If your present fixtures do not have individual shutoff valves, turn off the water at the main shutoff valve. Then, disconnect the supply lines to the fixture and attach pipe caps on the open ends. You can then open the main valve, which will restore water to the rest of the house. Pipe caps are available at most hardware stores.

If any fixture does not at present have individual hot and cold shutoff valves — except the toilet, which requires only one valve — it is an easy matter to add them when you replace the fixture. Stop valves and fittings for connecting them to the fixture are available in kit form from plumbing supply stores and most hardware stores.

Suppose you want to replace a bathroom lavatory; you should have little trouble with the code, because all you are doing is hooking up a new fixture to existing pipes. Chances are that you will not even need new adapters or fittings. If your old plumbing pipes are unattractive, you can hide them easily with a cabinet-type lavatory that also provides some additional storage space. For a wall-hung, leg-supported or pedestal-type lavatory, however, you can replace any unattractive pipes or drains with chrome ones.

Replacing a Wall-Mounted Lavatory

A wall-mounted lavatory is supported by a metal hanger that is anchored by screws to a wood support in the wall. Although the lavatory may have metal legs at the front corners, these legs provide only additional support and do not carry the entire weight of the fixture.

If you are replacing an old lavatory with one of the same style, the existing hanger bracket will serve. However, if your new lavatory is of a different style, you may need a bracket specifically designed for it. When you buy the new fixture, find out from the dealer whether you will need a new mounting bracket.

To remove the old lavatory and install a new one, follow this general procedure: Shut off the water supply. If there are no shutoff valves at the fixture, turn off the main shutoff valve. Place a bucket under the lavatory's trap and unscrew the clean-out plug if the trap has one. The water in the trap will pour into the bucket. If the trap does not have a plug, proceed carefully with the next step. Loosen the two slip nuts that hold the trap in place. If you intend to reuse these fittings, wrap tape around them and use a smooth-jawed adjustable wrench to remove them; a pipe wrench will damage their surfaces. When the nuts have been loosened, pull down on the trap to free it. If the trap has no drain plug, remove the trap carefully and empty the water in the trap into the bucket.

Use a basin wrench to loosen the supply-line coupling nuts from the faucet studs, or shanks, if you cannot reach the nuts with another type of wrench. If the nuts are too rusted or corroded to turn, use a hacksaw to cut the supply pipes. With an adjustable wrench, loosen the nuts that couple the fixture supply pipes to the shutoff valves or to the wall supply pipes. Then, remove the fixture supply pipes.

When all supply and drain lines are disconnected, lift the lavatory straight up from the mounting bracket and place it on the floor, face down, atop an old rug or other padding.

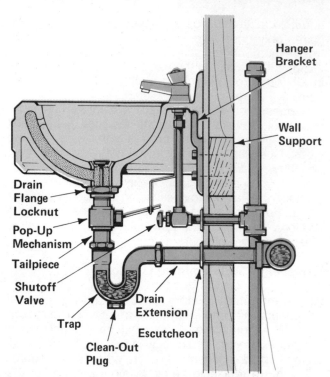

Shown here is a typical wall-mounted lavatory with a pop-up drain and shutoff valves.

Labels on the diagram:
- Hanger Bracket
- Wall Support
- Drain Flange Locknut
- Pop-Up Mechanism
- Tailpiece
- Shutoff Valve
- Trap
- Drain Extension
- Escutcheon
- Clean-Out Plug

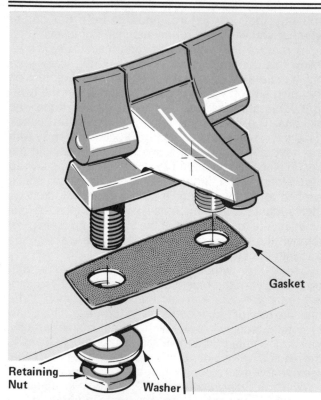

Before mounting the lavatory's new faucet and spout assembly, apply plumber's putty around the base or install the gasket supplied with the unit.

Labels on the diagram:
- Gasket
- Retaining Nut
- Washer

You can now remove the nuts that hold the faucets in place and remove the faucet assembly. Be sure to keep the washers. (If you are also replacing the faucets, there is no need to remove the old ones.) Disconnect the pop-up drain linkage, if present. Finally, loosen the slip nut that holds the drain flange and the tailpiece of the drainpipe in place and remove both.

Now it is time to install your new wall-mounted lavatory. If necessary, remove the old hanger bracket from the wall and attach a new bracket to the wall. Also, if you wish to install shutoff valves, do so now, following the procedure outlined in the section "Installing a Shutoff Valve" in this chapter. Then, proceed with the installation of the lavatory.

Place the new lavatory on the floor on its side atop padding to avoid damaging it. Apply plumber's putty (or the gasket supplied with a new faucet and spout assembly) around the base of the faucet and spout assembly, and put it in place. On the underside of the lavatory, screw the retaining nuts onto the faucet shanks. Install the drain flange and tailpiece. Tighten all nuts with a wrench. Attach the pop-up drain linkage. Connect the supply line sections to the faucet shanks and tighten their coupling nuts with a wrench.

Lift the lavatory and slide it straight down over the mounting bracket. Connect the supply lines to the stop valves or wall supply pipes. Then, install the trap. Finally, turn on the water supply and check all connections for any leakage.

Installing a Counter-Top Lavatory

Counter-top lavatories may be surface-mounted or frame-mounted. The two types have identical plumbing hookups, however.

A surface-mounted lavatory supports itself by a lip around the edge of the basin. To remove such a fixture, simply disconnect all the plumbing lines as you would for a wall-mounted lavatory. Use a thin knife to break the seal around the lip, and then lift out the lavatory. To install a surface-mounted lavatory, obtain the proper mounting sealant from your plumbing supply dealer, apply it liberally under the lip of the lavatory, then lower the lavatory gently into place. Do not press it down tightly. Using a damp cloth, immediately wipe up any sealant that squeezes out from under the lip. The plumbing lines may be reconnected after the sealant has cured for about four hours.

A frame-mounted lavatory is held in place by clips and a band-like metal frame that circles the edge of the lavatory. Care must be taken during removal and installation of a frame-mounted lavatory so that it does not fall through the opening in the counter top. To replace a frame-mounted lavatory, follow this procedure:

Shut off the water supply at the fixture's shutoff valves or at the main shutoff. If there is a clean-out at the bottom of the lavatory's trap, place a bucket under it and remove the plug. If there is none, you will have to empty the water after you remove the trap. Wrap tape around the trap slip nuts and use a smooth-jawed adjustable wrench to loosen the slip nuts at each end of the trap. Pull down on the trap to remove it.

Use a basin wrench to loosen the supply-line coupling nuts from the faucet shanks and an adjustable wrench to loosen the nuts at the shutoff valves. Remove the supply lines.

Drop a loop of lightweight rope, such as clothesline rope, through the lavatory's drain hole. Insert a length of wood through the top end of the loop so that the ends of the wooden piece rest on the counter top. Insert a small wood block through the bottom end of the loop and twist the block until it is wedged tightly against the bottom of the drain tailpiece. This arrangement will hold the lavatory in place as you remove the supporting clips.

Unscrew the bolts that hold the supporting clips in place under the lavatory and remove the clips. As you support the lavatory from below with one hand, turn the wood block with the other hand to untwist the rope. When the rope is loose enough, remove the block and let it drop. Then lower and remove the lavatory. Disconnect the pop-up drain linkage and remove the tailpiece and drain flange by loosening the locknut that holds them in place.

If you plan to use the lavatory's faucet and spout assembly again, use a pair of pliers or a wrench to loosen the retaining nuts on the faucet shanks. Remove the nuts and lift off the assembly. Finally, insert a thin knife blade between the edge of the metal support rim and the counter top to break the putty seal, and remove the rim.

If you want to do so, you can install shutoff valves for the fixture at this time. Then, to install the faucet and spout assembly on the new lavatory, apply plumber's putty (or a gasket) to the base of the faucet and spout assembly and press the assembly into place. Screw the retaining nuts onto the faucet shanks and tighten them with a wrench. Attach the water supply pipes to the faucet shanks, install the drain flange and drain tailpiece, and connect the pop-up drain linkage.

Then, put a continuous bead of plumber's putty around the inside and outside lips of the mounting rim. Position the rim on the edge of the hole in the counter and press the rim firmly in place. Use a damp cloth to wipe away any excess putty that may squeeze out.

You can now use the rope-and-block technique described in the removal procedure to support the new lavatory in place. Put the mounting clips in place, spacing them evenly around the perimeter of the lavatory, and turn the bolts down firmly. Remove the rope-and-block support apparatus.

Connect the water supply lines to the shutoff valves and replace the trap assembly. Finally, restore the water supply.

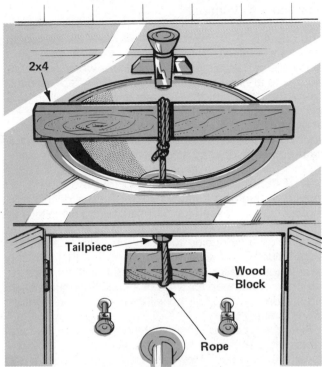

Shown is the rope-and-block apparatus used to hold the lavatory in place while you remove the supporting clips.

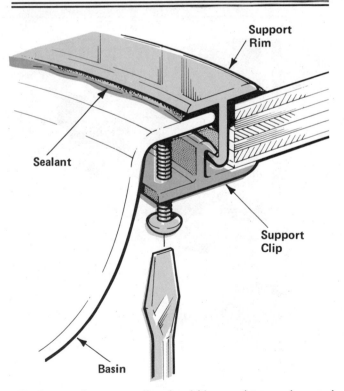

The lavatory's support clips should be evenly spaced around the perimeter of the lavatory. The bolts should then be turned down firmly.

Replacing a Bathtub

The bathtub is the most difficult of the basic bathroom fixtures to replace. In fact, if you have a recessed tub, there are certain circumstances under which it is inadvisable to attempt to replace it yourself. A recessed tub has a flange, or lip, that usually is attached directly to the wall studs. The wall finishing materials — wallboard or plaster, tile, etc. — are applied over the flange. So, if your present recessed tub extends the full width of your bathroom, the tub may actually be longer than the bathroom is wide. Such circumstances may require that part of the wall be cut away and that the tub be removed through an adjacent room. Before deciding to replace your recessed tub yourself, take a close look to determine exactly what removal and replacement may entail. You may decide to leave the work to a professional plumber, after all. If you do decide that you can handle the situation yourself, remember that the existing drain is plumbed for a tub of a specific width. Installing a wider or narrower tub will require some relocation of the drain.

Removing a tub-on-legs usually is much simpler than removing a recessed tub, because the drain connections are exposed. However, replacing it with a recessed tub will require matching the drain opening to the new tub. Also, you will have to remove the wall

If you are able to reach the drain connections through an access panel, loosen the slip nuts that join the overflow pipe and the drain elbow to the main drainpipe.

material below the edge of the new tub to attach the tub flange to the studs.

The following general procedures are for removing and installing a recessed tub. However, you will have to adapt them to the design of the tub you are working with. If you are removing a tub-on-legs, removal of the drain connections are basically the same as for a recessed tub.

Turn off the water at the main shutoff valve. Remove the screws that hold the tub's overflow plate/stopper control in place. Remove the overflow plate and pull out the stopper control mechanism. Then remove the access panel in the opposite side of the wall at the drain end of the tub. If there is no such panel, you have two options. First, you can cut into the wall where the access panel should be. (After you have replaced the tub, you can install a removable panel in place over the opening.) Second, you can disconnect the tub from the drain pipe through the drain opening in the tub itself.

If you are able to reach the drain connections through an access opening, use a wrench or adjustable pliers to loosen the slip nuts that join the overflow pipe and the drain elbow to the main drainpipe. Remove the overflow pipe.

If there is no access opening, unscrew and remove the drain flange from inside the tub. Then, use pliers to remove the sleeve inside the tub drain opening. That will disconnect the tub from the drain elbow.

Remove the faucets and tub spout from the wall. Remove the nipples (short lengths of pipe) to which the faucets and spout were attached, and remove anything else that projects beyond the face of the studs and might interfere with removal of the tub.

Now, free the tub flanges. Using a cold chisel and a hammer, cut away a 4-inch-high section of the wall surface all the way around the tub. Some tubs are anchored to the studs with nails or screws. If your tub is so anchored, remove all the fasteners.

Insert a pry bar under the tub skirt at one end of the tub. Raise the end of the tub and place a small wedge under it. Repeat this process until a 1x2-inch wood strip can be placed under that end of the tub to hold it off the floor. Then repeat the procedure at the other end of the tub.

At this point, you will need help. If your tub is cast iron, you will probably need two assistants to safely move the tub out. Two people can handle a steel tub. In either case have a dolly handy to move the tub through the house to the outdoors.

Your helpers (or helper) should pull outward on the tub while you use a pry bar to force the tub away from the studs. Work the tub outward until there is space behind it for you to stand. Then get behind it and tilt the tub forward until it is standing on the front skirt. Continue to work the tub out of the recess until it can be lifted onto the dolly. You will find it easier to lift the tub onto a dolly that is lying flat than it is to stand the tub on end and then get the foot of the dolly under the tub.

Unpack your new tub well in advance of the time when you want to install it. If installation instructions have not been included, ask the dealer for a set. You will require specific instructions, because there is no standard installation method. And, since your dealer may have to order the instruction sheet from the tub manufacturer, you will want to allow as much time as possible so that you will have it when you are ready to begin work.

Some enameled steel and fiberglass tubs come with foam padding cemented to the bottom. This padding actually supports the tub. When the tub is properly leveled (with the help of a carpenter's level), the padding supports the tub at a height that leaves about a ⅛-inch gap between the floor and the bottom of the tub apron or skirt.

If one of these padded tubs cannot be leveled, it might be necessary to remove a section of the floor under the tub, place shims on the joists, and then replace the flooring. Under no circumstances, however, should you attempt to put shims under the padding.

Some tubs are supported at the ends and along the back by wood supports nailed to the studs. These supports must be perfectly leveled and placed at the exact height required for the tub involved. Some plastic tubs have flange extensions that must be drilled at stud locations for nails or screws. Other tubs require special clips that fit over the tub flange and are nailed to the studs. And, some tubs with thick flanges make it necessary to nail shim strips to the stud faces so that there is a level base for the wallboard that has to extend down over the tub flange. Also, the width of the offset below the flange on some tubs dictates the thickness of wallboard that can be installed over the flange. So, you can see why you must have the manufacturer's instructions to install your new tub properly.

There are, however, some general rules to consider before attempting to install a recessed or corner tub:

1. Use a carpenter's level to be sure the tub and/or the tub flange supports are level. Do not rely on "eyeball" leveling.
2. Place a mineral fiber or glass fiber insulation blanket under steel or plastic tubs that do not come with padding. This insulation will reduce noise when the tub is filled. Use enough insulation to pack the space, but not enough to support the tub.
3. Wallboard must be installed over the tub flange, but it must not touch the tub rim. If it does touch the rim, it will soak up water, which will damage the board core. To avoid this problem, place ⅛-inch wood strips around the rim to insure proper separation when you install the wallboard. When the wallboard is in place, pull out the strips and fill the gap with caulking or sealant material.

If your local building code requires special water-resistive wallboard for tub and shower en-

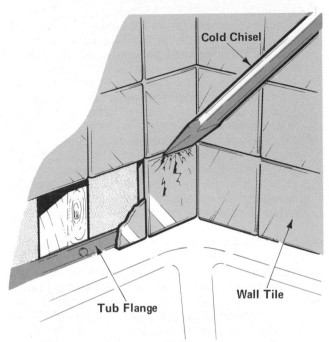

To free the tub's flanges, use a cold chisel and hammer to cut away a 4-inch-high section of the wall surface all the way around the tub.

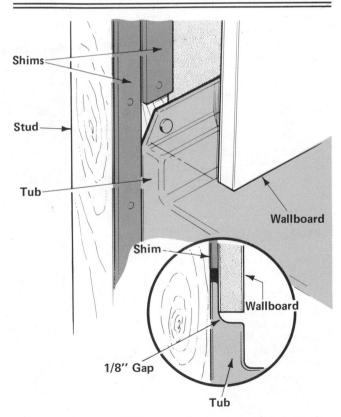

Some tubs with thick flanges make it necessary to nail shim strips to the stud faces so that there is a level base for wallboard that has to extend down over the tub flange.

63

closures, be sure to get the special sealant that goes with it. Whenever this type of wallboard is cut, the cut edge must be painted with the sealant to preserve the water-resistive properties of the core. You should be aware that this type of gypsum board is intended for walls only, not for ceilings. On ceilings in high-humidity areas, this board is less sag-resistant than conventional wallboard.

4. You can replace the faucets and spout and connect the tub to the drain — in order to put the tub back into service — before you repair the wall area around the rim of the tub. However, because the rim of the tub will not yet be sealed, you must avoid splashing water into the wall cavity.

LAVATORY AND TUB STOPPERS

You flip up a lever at the end of the tub or you raise the lifter handle between two faucets on the lavatory basin, and in both cases the stopper, or plug, closes the drain. Who gives these stoppers a second thought? Yet, when a plumbing problem occurs and you need to get into the drain, you give that stopper plenty of thought

because that is when you must get the tub or basin stopper out of your way.

One common lavatory basin stopper is a pop-up hollow cylinder attached to a rod that sticks out into the drainpipe. When you pull on the lifter, a lever pivots a ball that causes the rod to go down and pull the stopper down with it. Since the top of the cylinder is closed, the water stays in the basin when the cylinder is down; the drain is closed.

A pop-up hollow-cylinder stopper is easy to remove. Just apply a slight downward pressure, twist it a quarter-turn (most of them twist clockwise, but some go the other way), and pull it out. Remove the basin stopper at least once a month, and clean out the hair and whatever else is caught in it. In addition, corrosion or dirt can collect around the lip of the stopper, allowing water to slowly drain away. You may not even be able to see any residue, but removal and cleaning of the stopper should stop the seepage.

Some pop-up stoppers rest on the end of the pivot rod; they can be removed simply by raising the stopper to its open position and lifting the stopper from the drain. Another type of pop-up stopper has a loop in its

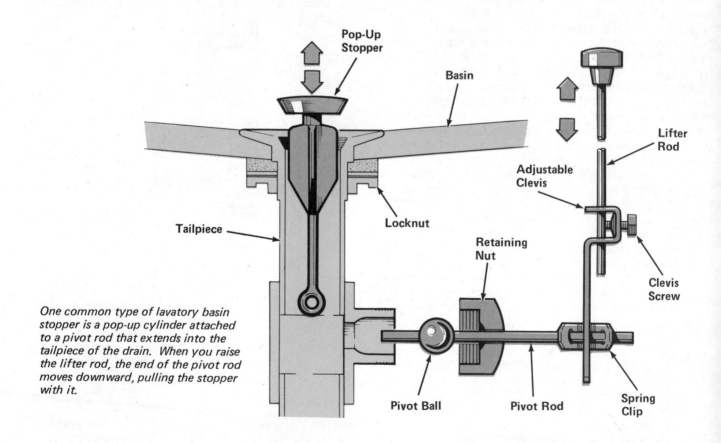

One common type of lavatory basin stopper is a pop-up cylinder attached to a pivot rod that extends into the tailpiece of the drain. When you raise the lifter rod, the end of the pivot rod moves downward, pulling the stopper with it.

base that engages the end of the pivot rod; you must disengage the pivot rod by pulling it partially or completely out of the drain before this kind of stopper can be removed.

A popular tub stopper system, called the trip-lever, has no *visible* stopper. All that you see in the tub is a strainer-type cover on the drain opening. When you flip the lever, the trip-lever system closes the drain by lowering a hollow metal plug inside the drain into a position that blocks the outflow of water. The lever itself is mounted on an open plate that is designed to also accommodate any tub overflow. The plate acts as the cover of the opening on the overflow pipe. To remove a trip-lever system stopper in order to clean the overflow tube, take out the screws in the plate and lift the entire assembly straight out; it goes back in the same way.

A pop-up stopper in a tub consists basically of a trip-lever system with an added feature. The pop-up drain assembly has a spring — instead of a metal plug — at the base of the lever linkage. The spring rests on one end of a rocker arm; the other end of the arm is attached to the stopper itself. When the lever mounted on the overflow plate is depressed, the spring is raised, allowing that end of the rocker arm to move upward. The other end of the arm is simultaneously lowered, thus closing the drain.

A pop-up drain stopper in a tub can be easily removed by levering it to its open position and pulling the stopper and its arm linkage out of the drain. This stopper usually has an O-ring under its lip. If the drain leaks, the O-ring can be easily replaced. The lever part of the assembly is removed in the same way as a basic trip-lever system.

The fact that a lavatory or tub stopper does not seal properly and allows water to slowly drain away does not necessarily mean that the stopper must be replaced. The cause may be only a collection of dirt and residue around the stopper seal; periodic cleaning takes care of that problem. Another possibility is that the O-ring or other flexible seal under the lip of the stopper is worn or damaged. Replacing the seal is easy enough; some can be slipped on from above, but others must be worked on from the bottom of the stopper, which requires removal of the assembly. A third possible cause for seepage past the stopper seal is that the unit may not be properly adjusted. Various kinds of linkage systems are used for operating a pop-up stopper, but you will find at least one adjustment point and often two or three in any system. They may include a lift rod with adjustable clevis, a clevis with perforations spaced out at intervals to receive a pop-up pivot rod at the best location, a threaded rod and locknut arrangement, adjustable link pins or some similar mechanism. By moving and resecuring these parts in relation to one another, you should be able to effect a tighter fit between the pop-up plug seal and the drain flange.

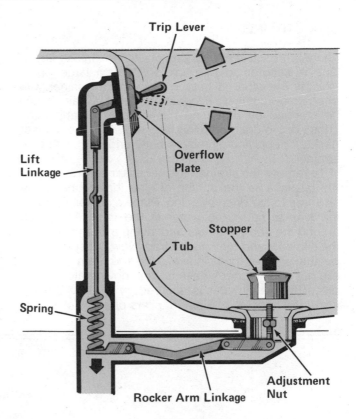

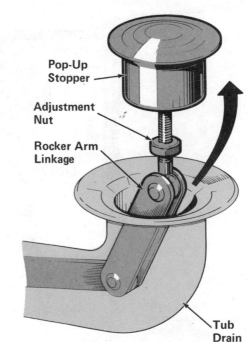

The tub pop-up stopper has a spring that rests on one end of a rocker arm; the other end of the rocker arm is attached to the stopper itself. When the trip lever is raised, the spring is depressed, forcing one end of the rocker arm down; the other end raises the stopper in the tub. Usually there is a nut at the stopper for height adjustment.

SINK STRAINERS

There are basically two types of kitchen sink strainers. One is secured to the sink drain by a large metal locknut; the other is held in place by a retainer with three screws. If there is a leak around the drain, it may be stopped by removing the strainer, cleaning the edges of the drain opening, and replacing the strainer gasket or applying plumber's putty under the lip of the strainer.

To remove the strainer, it is necessary to first remove the tailpiece — the portion of pipe that connects the sink trap to the drain opening. Place a container under the sink to catch the water in the trap. Wrap tape around the trap's slip nuts and, using a wrench, loosen the slip nuts and remove the trap. Now, loosen the slip nut that secures the tailpiece to the sink drain; allow the slip nut and strainer sleeve to slide down onto the tailpiece. If your strainer is secured by a large locknut, insert the handles of a pair of pliers or some other tool

into the sink drain to prevent the strainer from turning. Use a large pipe wrench to loosen the locknut. If a large wrench is not available, brace a piece of wooden dowel into one of the locknut's notches, and tap the end of the dowel with a hammer to loosen the locknut. After you remove the locknut, along with the metal and rubber washers under it, gently tap the underside of the strainer until it pops loose.

To re-install the old strainer after cleaning or to install a new strainer, reverse the procedure, but make sure you do not overtighten the locknut or it may damage the strainer's parts. Before inserting the strainer into the drain hole in the sink, clean off any old putty from the basin or strainer flange and apply fresh plumber's putty around the edge of the drain hole. Place the strainer in position; use a damp cloth to wipe away excess putty.

To reconnect the tailpiece and trap, place the strainer sleeve over the end of the tailpiece and secure the tailpiece to the strainer by tightening its slip nut.

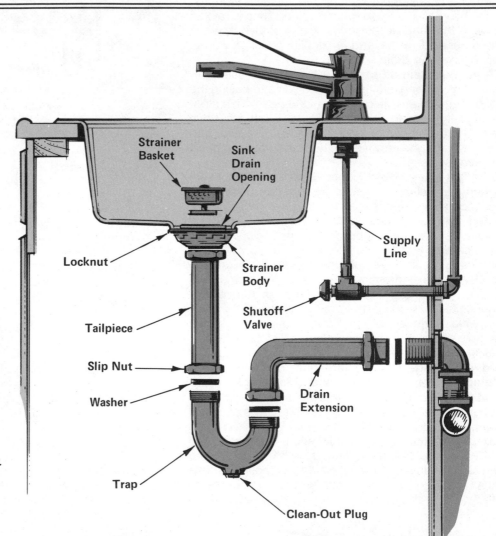

To remove the strainer body under the sink drain opening, it is necessary to remove the tailpiece—the portion of the drainpipe that connects the sink trap to the drain opening.

Position the trap and tighten the slip nuts that secure the trap to the tailpiece and to the drain extension. Turn on the water and check the drain, strainer, tailpiece, and trap for signs of leaks. If there are any leaks, re-check the connections and tighten them.

If the strainer is fastened by means of a retainer, unscrew each of the retainer's three screws after removing the drain tailpiece. The strainer can then be pried out of the drain. Reverse the procedure to replace the original strainer or to install a new one.

TUB-SHOWER DIVERTERS

The diverter in a tub-shower combination directs the flow of water to either the tub spout or the shower head. There are two kinds: the tub-spout diverter and the diverter valve. The tub-spout diverter is a simple mechanical gate within the spout itself. With the operating knob down, the gate is open and water flows from the spout; with the knob up, the gate is closed and water is forced to flow from the shower head. The diverter valve, usually wall-mounted, operates much like a faucet valve, and turning the handle changes the internal flow of water from the tub supply pipe to the shower supply pipe, or vice versa.

If a tub-spout diverter leaks or does not operate properly, it must be replaced with a new spout and diverter assembly; they are not repairable. You can remove the old spout by turning it counterclockwise with a wrench or a stick of wood wedged into the spout opening. If it is difficult to turn, be very careful not to apply so much pressure that pipe or fittings inside the wall are damaged; if you have access to the supply pipe, fit a wrench to the pipe and apply equal counterforce. After removing the old spout, clean the pipe threads and apply plumber's joint compound or tape. Screw the new spout on clockwise until it is positioned correctly and as snug as you can get it by hand. If you need to turn it just a little beyond that point to align correctly, a strap wrench or a stick of wood in the spout opening will do the job. But make sure you do not over-tighten.

A malfunctioning diverter valve — one that causes poor or erratic flow, incomplete diversion from tub to shower, difficult or squeaky operation, or leaks around the stem — can often be repaired in much the same manner as a stem faucet. Remove the handle screw, handle, trim plate, and large packing nut. You may need a deep socket wrench to loosen this nut if it is recessed in the wall. Remove the stem or cartridge; clean and lube the stem parts with petroleum jelly. Replace any O-rings, packing, or washers that are worn; check the valve seat and threads for signs of damage. After replacing or repairing necessary components, reassemble the unit. If this does not result in satisfactory performance, you will probably have to replace the entire valve.

SHOWER HEADS

Shower heads are subject to several problems. Leaks, for instance, can occur where the head connects to the shower arm (the curved, chrome-plated pipe that protrudes from the wall) or at the connection between the shower head body and the swivel ball. If the arm connection leaks, unscrew the entire shower head from the pipe, using a pair of strap wrenches if necessary. If you use other types of wrenches, tape the pipe to avoid scratching it. Clean the arm threads and coat them with plumber's joint compound or a wrap of plumber's joint tape. Screw the shower head back and hand-tighten it only. Remove any excess compound or tape. If the leak is at the swivel, unscrew the shower head body from the swivel ball ring. You will find an O-ring or a similar seal inside. Replace it and screw the shower head back in place.

Problems can also be caused by grit or sediment lodging in the head or from a build-up of scale or mineral deposits. The solution is to remove the shower head body at the swivel ball, strip it completely apart and start cleaning. Soaking in vinegar may be necessary for some parts, scraping for others. Be careful, though, not to scratch or gouge anything. If the shower head is of the adjustable-spray type, examine all of the moving parts carefully for signs of excessive wear. If the adjustment handle binds or does not work smoothly, or the internal cam is fouled up, usually the only solution is to replace the entire head.

Installation of a personal shower unit in an existing shower is a simple matter. You can remove the existing shower head from the shower arm, and couple the flexible hose of the personal shower unit directly to the arm, using a little plumber's joint compound or tape on the threads. Or, you can remove the existing shower head and screw an adapter fitting on in its place. The original shower head is then screwed back into one opening of the adaptor and the personal shower hose into the other. A small lever-operated valve diverts water from one to the other. In either case, the personal shower can be attached to a slide-bar mounted on the shower wall, or simply hung in a small bracket. Personal shower units bear a great deal of resemblance to both ordinary shower heads and sink spray heads, and servicing or cleaning them is usually a combination of procedures used for the other two.

CLEARING CLOGGED DRAINS

Of the two most common plumbing problems — dripping faucets and clogged drains — the latter is undoubtedly the one that receives the most attention. Most people fail to realize how much a drip costs them, but they all know the inconvenience as well as the mess that accompanies a sluggish drain. Even so, many people wait until the drain situation becomes dire

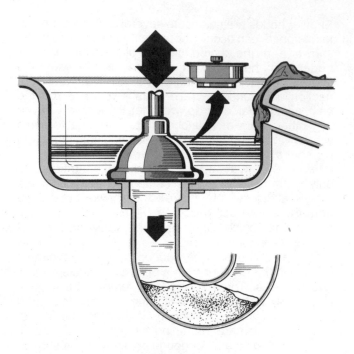

To unclog a sink or lavatory drain, you must cover the plunger's rubber cup with water and plug the fixture's vent opening with wet rags.

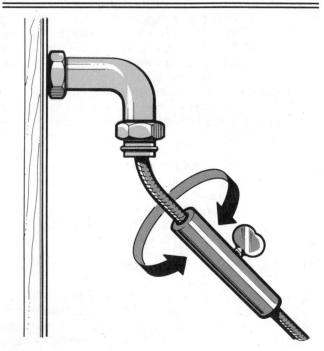

If the clog is not in the fixture's trap, insert a drain-and-trap auger into the drain extension that goes into the wall, and work the auger into the drainpipe.

— that is, when *no* water runs out — before they take corrective action.

When they do finally start their corrective action they usually fail. That is a result of their not knowing how to use one of the best drain-clearing tools of them all: the plumber's friend, or the rubber plunger. Working a plunger requires no special training or expertise, but if it is to do its job properly, you must know a few basic facts. Otherwise, you will follow the familiar syndrome: pump up and down two or three times, step back to see what happens, and then go on to other drain-clearing devices — or even call in a plumber — when the water fails to whoosh out the drain.

If you expect to clear a clogged drain with a plunger, the suction cup must be large enough to cover the drain opening completely. Second, the water in the sink or tub must cover the plunger's cup completely. Third — and undoubtedly the most neglected aspect of using this tool — you must block off all the other outlets between the drain and the blockage. If you fail to block off the outlets, all the pressure you create will be dissipated long before it can get to the clog.

For clogged lavatory, sink and tub drains, the following procedure should be used with the plunger: First, cover the overflow opening, or vent, in the basin (or tub) with a wet cloth. Most kitchen sinks do not have one; but if you are working on one of two side-by-side basins, you will have to plug the other basin's drain opening with wet cloths. In addition, there may yet be another drain outlet connected to the drain line you are working on that must be blocked as well; you will find that out, however, if the water starts backing up in the unsuspected outlet. For example, in homes that have two bathrooms back to back in adjacent rooms, there is a good chance that both are connected to the same drain. In such cases you must block the other basin at both its drain and overflow vent. Shower facilities seldom have overflow vents, but bathtubs have such vents, and laundry tubs may have two or three. You must cover all of them with wet cloths for your plunger to work properly.

Next, fill the clogged basin with enough water to cover the head of the plunger. Coat the lip of the plunger with petroleum jelly; this assures a better seal. *Slide* the plunger's cup over the drain opening. Then, rapidly pump the plunger up and down. You should feel the water move in and out of the drain. It is this back-and-forth water pressure that can eventually build up enough force to dislodge whatever is blocking the drain. After about a dozen strokes, jerk the plunger up quickly. The water should rush out. If it fails to do so, try the same procedure two or three more times before attempting another method.

If the plunger fails to free the clog in your drain, you will have to try another method. Many people often turn to a chemical drain opener — in either dry or liquid form. In a drain that is completely blocked, however, it

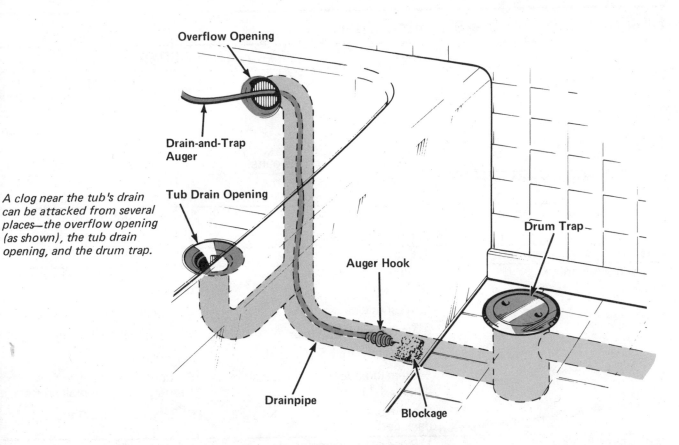

Overflow Opening

Drain-and-Trap Auger

Tub Drain Opening

Drum Trap

Auger Hook

Drainpipe

Blockage

A clog near the tub's drain can be attacked from several places—the overflow opening (as shown), the tub drain opening, and the drum trap.

is best not to use chemicals. For one thing, such powerful drain cleaners contain caustic agents that can harm fixtures, and if you must later remove a trap or clean-out to free the blockage, you will be exposed to the harmful solution.

Instead, your safest course is to resort to a drain-and-trap auger. To use it, remove the pop-up stopper or strainer from the clogged drain, and insert the auger wire into the opening. As you feed the flexible wire in, crank the handle of the device clockwise, loosening and then tightening the thumbscrew on the handle as you advance the wire. If the wire encounters something, move it back and forth while you turn the auger handle. Then, continue to turn the handle while withdrawing the auger slowly.

If the auger has cleared the drain of most of the debris inside, you can pour hot, soapy water into the drain to remove any remaining debris. If the auger failed to work, proceed to the trap to unclog the drain.

If the trap under the basin is equipped with a clean-out, remove the clean-out plug, catching the water in the trap in a bucket. You can use a wire coat hanger with a hook shaped in one end to attempt to reach the clog. However, if this fails, insert the wire from the drain-and-trap auger through the clean-out — work

toward the basin and toward the drainpipe to remove the blockage.

If the trap does not have a clean-out, remove the trap, following the procedure outlined in the section "Trap Replacement" in this chapter. With the trap removed, you can clean it out with a wire coat hanger and then with a stiff brush and hot, soapy water. Replace the trap if you have removed the clog. If the clog was not in the trap, insert the drain-and-trap auger into the drain extension that goes into the wall, and continue working the auger down into the drainpipe itself. You should be able to reach the blockage, unless it is in a section of the main drain.

If a bathtub drain is clogged and a plunger failed to clear the drain, use the drain-and-trap auger first through the tub drain opening. If unsuccessful, remove the overflow plate and insert the auger directly into the overflow pipe and down into the drainpipe.

NOTE: Some older bathtubs have a drum trap. Usually, it is found near the tub at floor level. Unscrew the lid of the drum trap counterclockwise with an adjustable wrench. Clean out the trap. If the debris is elsewhere, attempt to reach it through the drum trap with the drain-and-trap auger.

For floor drains, such as those in basements and

Sink and Tub Trouble-Shooting Chart

PROBLEMS	CAUSES	REPAIRS
Faucet drips	1. Faulty washer.	1. Replace washer. For single-handled faucet, install all parts in repair kit.
	2. Improper valve seat.	2. Use valve seat grinder to even seat, or replace seat.
	3. Worn stem or cartridge parts.	3. Replace stem assembly.
Hot water slows to trickle	1. Washer expands when hot.	1. Replace with proper, nonexpanding washer.
Leaks around faucet handle	1. Packing nut loose.	1. Tighten packing unit.
	2. Inadequate packing.	2. Replace packing.
Leaks around faucet spout	1. Faulty O-ring.	1. Replace O-ring.
Faucet makes noise	1. Wrong size washer.	1. Replace washer with one of proper size.
	2. Washer loose.	2. Tighten washer on stem.
	3. Valve seat clogged.	3. Clean residue from valve seat.
	4. Pipes too small or clogged.	4. Replace pipes.
	5. Stem threads binding against threads in faucet body.	5. Lubricate stem threads with petroleum jelly, or replace stem.
	6. Stem or body threads damaged.	6. Replace stem or faucet.
Drains overflowing	1. Pipes or trap clogged.	1. Use plunger or auger to clear pipes or trap.
Drain sluggish with sucking noises	1. Drain flow restricted.	1. Clean drain.
	2. Vent restricted.	2. Clean vent.
	3. Improper venting.	3. Install vent or larger vent.
Sink stopper does not retain water	1. Strainer damaged.	1. Replace strainer.
	2. Basket strainer seal faulty.	2. Replace basket strainer.
Lavatory or tub stopper does not retain water	1. O-ring or other stopper seal is worn.	1. Replace O-ring or other seal.
	2. Stopper pop-up linkage improperly adjusted.	2. Adjust linkage.
Moisture under fixture	1. Leaking trap joints.	1. Tighten trap slip nuts or clean-out plug.
	2. Leaking trap.	2. Replace trap.
	3. Leaking connections at fixture.	3. Tighten, or disassemble and repair.
	4. Leaking connections at shutoff valves.	4. Tighten, or disassemble and repair.
	5. Leaking seal at fixture drain.	5. Remove, clean, and reseal drain flange.
	6. Caulking seal around fixture rim faulty—splash water seeping.	6. Remove fixture as necessary and recaulk.

Sink and Tub Trouble-Shooting Chart (Continued)

PROBLEMS	CAUSES	REPAIRS
Water stream uneven or aeration level diminished on aerated faucet	1. Aerator clogged with grit, scale or sediment.	1. Disassemble aerator and clean.
Spray head does not function properly	1. Spray head body or lever malfunction.	1. Replace spray head.
	2. Spray head aerator clogged.	2. Disassemble and clean aerator.
	3. Hose damaged or connection is loose.	3. Repair or replace hose; tighten connections.
	4. Hose is clogged.	4. Remove blockage; replace hose, if necessary.
	5. Diverter valve clogged or damaged.	5. Disassemble and clean valve; if necessary, replace valve.
Tub-spout diverter leaks or is inoperative	1. Tub-spout diverter broken.	1. Replace spout-diverter assembly.
Tub-shower diverter valve malfunctioning	1. Washers, seals, packing, valve seat or threads worn.	1. Repair or replace appropriate components.
	2. Diverter valve damaged.	2. Replace valve.
Shower head leaks	1. Connection at arm loose or corroded.	1. Tighten; or remove head from arm, clean, coat with plumber's joint compound, and retighten.
	2. Swivel connection O-ring or other seal in poor condition.	2. Replace O-ring or other seal and retighten.
Shower head water flow restricted	1. Shower head clogged.	1. Disassemble and clean head.
Shower head adjustment handle binds or does not operate	1. Internal cam broken or other mechanical damage.	1. Replace shower head.

showers, a garden hose can be effective in unclogging drains, especially if the clog is not close to the opening. Attach the hose to a faucet, feed the hose into the drain as far as it will go, and jam rags around the hose at the opening. Then, turn the water on full force for a few moments.

If you suspect a clog is in the main drainpipe, locate the main clean-out; it is a Y-shaped fitting near the bottom of your home's soil stack or where the drain leaves your building. Place a large pail or container beneath the clean-out and prepare plenty of papers and rags around the site to soak up the backed-up water. Using a pipe wrench, unscrew the clean-out plug counterclockwise slowly, trying to control the flow of water that will seep from the clean-out. Once the flow has stopped and you have cleaned up the flooded site, insert the auger to remove the debris.

If you have not located the blockage, another place you can try is the house trap; this is a U-shaped fitting installed underground. You can locate it by finding two adjacent clean-out plugs in the floor, if the main drain runs under the floor. Again, place papers and rags around the site before opening the clean-out nearest to the sewer outside. If the clog is in the house trap or between the trap and the main clean-out, you should be able to remove it. But if water starts to flow out of the trap as you unscrew it, check quickly beyond the house trap with an auger. If you can remove the clog rapidly, do so. Otherwise, replace the trap plug and call in a professional to do the job.

If the clog is between the house trap and the main clean-out, insert the wire from the auger into the trap in the direction of the main clean-out. If the blockage is not in the trap but is in the drain itself, remove the

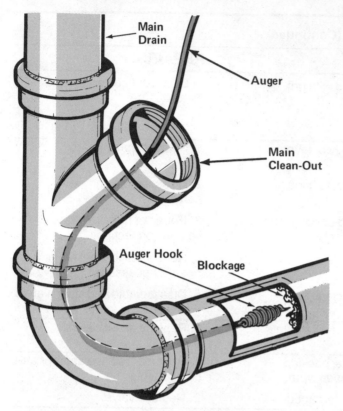

Main Drain

Auger

Main Clean-Out

Auger Hook

Blockage

A clog in the main drain may be reached from the main clean-out; it is a Y-shaped fitting near the bottom of your home's soil stack or where the drain leaves the building.

adjacent clean-out plug and try to reach the blockage from there with the auger.

Sometimes, a clog can collect in the soil stack — the vertical drainpipe that leads from the main drain and ends at the roof vent. If you have an auger that is long enough to reach the bottom of this pipe from the opening in the roof vent, you can try to free the blockage from the roof. In some cases, however, this can be risky work due to steeply pitched roofs, and it may be better to call in a professional to do this chore.

There is one type of drain clog that will not respond satisfactorily to plunger or auger. That is when the main drain outside of the building or a floor drain in your basement gets stopped up from tree roots that have grown in at the joints. The most effective solution is an electric rooter that is inserted into the pipe and cuts away roots from the pipe walls as it moves along.

You can rent one of these power augers at a tool-rental firm. You must feed the auger cable into the clean-out opening closest to the blockage. When the device's cutting head encounters roots, you should be able to feel the cable strain. Keep feeding the cable slowly until you feel a breakthrough; then go over the area once again. Remove the cable slowly and run water from a garden hose through the pipe to wash away the root cuttings. Before you return the power auger to the rental firm, replace the clean-out plug and flush a toilet several times. When you are convinced that the drain is clear of tree roots, you can clean the cable and return the machine.

The house trap is a U-shaped fitting installed underground. You can locate it by finding two adjacent clean-out plugs in the floor. Blockage between the trap and the main clean-out can be reached by removing the plug closest to the main clean-out.

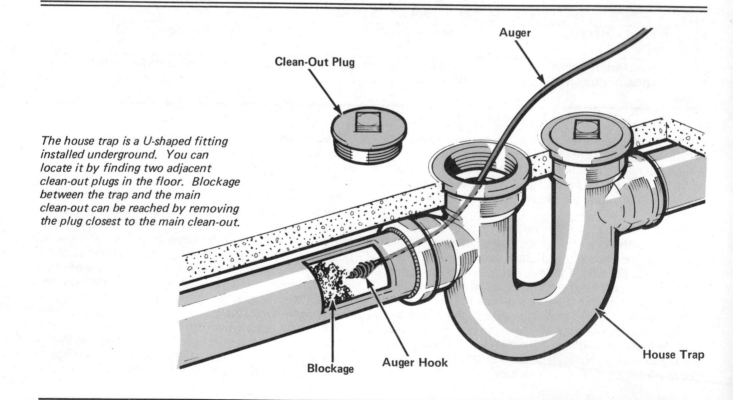

Clean-Out Plug

Auger

Blockage

Auger Hook

House Trap

Plumbing-Related Appliances

While everyone knows that water and electricity do not mix, modern engineering has come up with convenience devices that use the plumbing and electrical systems to reduce the time and effort required to wash clothes, wash dishes, and handle garbage. These are the plumbing-related appliances in your home — clothes washer, dishwasher, and garbage disposer — and you should know how they operate, how to fix them, and how to install replacement models if that should become necessary.

Of course, the fact that these appliances are marvels of engineering efficiency does not negate the basic principle that water and electricity can make a lethal combination if you are not extremely careful. **Caution:** Whenever you propose to tackle an appliance maintenance task, repair, or new installation, be sure that you first disconnect the appliance from its power source. Either pull the plug, remove the proper fuse, or trip the correct circuit breaker for the electrical circuit involved.

As long as you remember this basic safety principle, you can do a great deal of the servicing that your plumbing-related appliances require without endangering yourself. Naturally, by performing these tasks yourself — and by hooking up new appliances yourself — you can save yourself a great deal of money.

GARBAGE DISPOSERS

Garbage disposers are not usually temperamental appliances — they will grind just about anything you put into them. The most expensive models can even handle bones, corncobs, and seafood shells. Some day, however, you may put something in your garbage disposer that it cannot grind — bottle caps, tin can, glass, crockery, rag, string, paper, cardboard, rubber, plastic, cigarette filters, and so on — and the disposer will let you know of its indigestion by ceasing its operations.

You can cure disposer jams when you understand exactly how the appliance works. Contrary to what most people think, the blades in a garbage disposer are not sharp and they are not designed to cut up the waste (though they can do a terrible job on fingers).

Instead, the blades, or impellers, pivot on a flywheel, battering the waste and slinging it against the shredder and cutter surfaces of the unit. The flywheel spins at a rate of about 1,700 revolutions per minute, but it will come to a sudden halt if particles of hard matter get lodged between moving parts.

You can usually clear such jams quickly and easily through one simple procedure. Once you make sure that your garbage disposer is turned off, insert the end of a large wooden spoon handle, angle it against one of the impeller blades, and pry. The idea is to use the spoon handle as a lever to get particles out from where they are lodged under the moving parts. Eventually, you will feel the impeller give — although you may have to repeat the procedure several times — and you can then withdraw the spoon handle. Once you clear the blockage, push the disposer reset button (it trips automatically when a jam occurs), and you are ready to feed more waste into the unit.

Some disposers have a crank of some sort that fits into a socket in the bottom of the unit and lets you turn the flywheel plate in reverse. Deluxe models often have an automatic reversing mechanism that you operate merely by flipping the switch off and then on again. Whether done manually or automatically, however, the purpose of the reverse action is the same: to loosen the clog.

Although you should be able to clear any clog in your disposer without calling for professional assistance, there is really no reason to get into such a predicament in the first place. Be kind to your disposer; refrain from inserting objects that it will not be able to shred. If you are ever in doubt as to whether a particular substance should go into the disposer, play it safe until you know for sure and place the questionable material in your garbage pail instead. You may occasionally get away with depositing some of the things on the forbidden list, but eventually you will damage the disposer or clog the sink's drain — or both.

Always use cold water when you run your garbage disposer. Many people turn on the hot water, thinking that the hotter the water the better the grease will drain

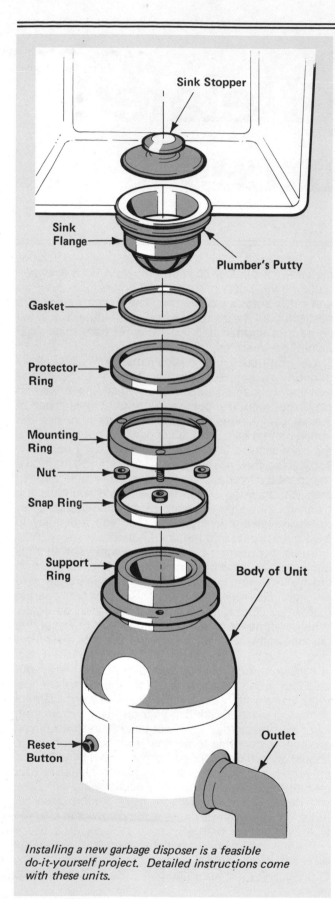

Sink Stopper

Sink Flange

Plumber's Putty

Gasket

Protector Ring

Mounting Ring

Nut

Snap Ring

Support Ring

Body of Unit

Reset Button

Outlet

Installing a new garbage disposer is a feasible do-it-yourself project. Detailed instructions come with these units.

away. Cold water, however, lets the grease congeal into tiny solid globules that can then be washed down the drain. Hot water only melts the grease, which then coats both the disposer and the drainpipes.

As grease builds up on the interior walls of the disposer, food particles collect there and cause unpleasant odors. Be careful, though, about using drain cleaners in your disposer unit. Never put regular drain-cleaning chemicals down your kitchen disposer. There are cleaners that are made specifically for disposers, and you should use only those types that are labeled as safe for use in garbage disposers. Such cleaners contain a petroleum distillate that can degrease, unclog, clean, and deodorize the unit.

Unless your disposer unit really needs a chemical cleaning, you might try this deodorizing technique. Fill the disposer about three quarters full of ice cubes, turn the unit on, and ignore the loud noises. Ice can help scrape off the food residue that clings to the disposer's walls. When all the ice is chewed up, flush the unit with cold water. Finally, drop in half of a lemon and let the disposer chew it up.

Preventive maintenance is about the limit of what the do-it-yourselfer can do in terms of food waste disposer repairs (although repair kits are available for some units in the event that an impeller blade comes loose). Most units are sealed and cannot be repaired easily. If you decide that your garbage disposer needs repair, you are probably wisest to call the authorized repair station for the brand you own.

Installing a Garbage Disposer

If you do not already have one, installing a new garbage disposer certainly constitutes a feasible do-it-yourself project. You will get detailed installation instructions with your new disposer, but here is the typical procedure required to add a disposer to your kitchen sink:

Begin by removing the sink's tailpiece and trap. (See the section entitled "Trap Replacement" for detailed information.) Also remove the sink drain flange, as well as any sealing material or gaskets. Clean the area around the drain opening in the sink. Now, place a ring of plumber's putty around the underside of the new sink flange, and insert the flange into the drain opening in the sink. Press — do *not* rotate — the flange in place. Remove any excess putty from around the flange.

From below the sink, slip the gasket over the underside of the sink flange, followed by the protector ring with the flat side up. The mounting ring — with three threaded pins screwed into it — follows the protector ring. While holding these parts in place above the groove on the flange, push the snap ring up along the flange, until it snaps into the groove. **Caution:** If you spread the snap ring, it can become too loose to hold in place around the groove. You may find it slow going to push the snap ring in place, but it *will* go. Make sure it fits firmly in the groove.

The threaded pins have slots for a screwdriver; they must be uniformly tightened against the protector ring to hold it and the gasket snugly against the bottom of the flange. Tighten the slotted pins evenly, keeping the mounting ring level and tight.

Now, lift the disposer and put it in place. Match the holes in the top of the disposer with the threaded pins, but before tightening the nuts that hold the disposer in place, make sure that its outlet pipe faces in the right direction for its connection to the drainpipe outlet. Tighten the nuts.

Now you are ready to hook up the trap to the disposer's outlet pipe. Use the slip nuts and washers; remember that the parts of the trap — the tailpiece, trap, and drain extension — can usually be maneuvered so that they will fit together. You may, however, have to buy and install some extra or replacement drain sections to complete a proper trap assembly. NOTE: On double-basin sinks, a common trap for both the disposer and the other basin is acceptable.

Check the disposer to see if any tools, screws or other materials have been dropped inside. Then, plug in the unit or install the switch and other wiring, following the manufacturer's directions and your local electrical code. Finally, test the disposer and check for leaks.

CLOTHES WASHERS

An automatic clothes washer probably constitutes the greatest labor-saving, plumbing-related appliance in

Garbage Disposer Trouble-Shooting Chart

PROBLEMS	CAUSES	REPAIRS
Caution: *Disconnect electrical power to disposer before inspecting or repairing.*		
Disposer fails to operate	1. Power outage.	1. Call power company.
	2. Circuit breaker tripped or fuse blown on circuit.	2. Clear circuit; reset circuit breaker or replace fuse.
	3. Overload device tripped.	3. Clear impeller if necessary; press reset button.
	4. Nondisposable substance or object jamming disposer.	4. Remove substance or object; insert large wooden spoon handle and pry against jammed impeller. Turn flywheel with crank (manual-reverse models). Flip switch off and then on (auto-reverse models).
	5. Defective relay switch, capacitor or motor.	5. Repair or replace disposer.
Disposer emits foul odor	1. Grease buildup—caused by using hot water to flush unit—traps food particles.	1. Apply drain cleaner specifically made for disposer, or fill disposer 3/4 full of ice and turn on unit to crush; then flush with cold water. Add half of lemon, turn unit on, and flush with cold water.
Disposer leaks	1. Loose sink flange connections.	1. Check connections and tighten.
	2. Impeller or seals leaking.	2. Call service technician.
Disposer makes excessive noise	1. Foreign object in disposer.	1. Remove foreign object.
Water fails to flow out	1. Clogged drain line.	1. Clear drain line; use only cleaner specifically made for disposer.
	2. Worn shredder.	2. Call service technician.

the home. A complete discussion of how one operates and how to fix one when it stops working is beyond the scope of this book, but you should have an idea of the plumbing problems that can arise in an automatic clothes washer. Moreover, if you know how to install a new unit, you can save yourself a good deal of money.

Most of the plumbing problems that occur in an automatic clothes washer have something to do with the water-inlet valves. These valves are operated by solenoids that raise plungers to allow water to flow into the machine and that lower plungers when the water flow is supposed to be shut off. The number of solenoids depends on the number of water-temperature selections on the clothes washer. There may be one (hot only), two (hot and cold), or three (hot, cold, and warm — a mixture of hot and cold water) solenoids. If one or more solenoids malfunction, the kind of water controlled by the solenoids will not enter the machine.

There are, however, other causes for water failing to flow into your clothes washer. In addition to the solenoid, the water-inlet valve itself may be defective. If it is, you must replace the valve. In cases where both the solenoid and the water-inlet valve are in good working order, the problem may simply be that a water-inlet hose is kinked or that the faucet to which the hose is connected may have been turned off for one reason or another. You can, of course, repair such difficulties merely by straightening the hose or opening the closed valve.

A somewhat more involved procedure is required, however, if none of the above solutions gets the water to flow. Disconnect the water-inlet hoses at the faucets and at the machine's water-inlet valves, and check the filter screens at both locations. It is quite possible that sand, rust or sediment could be clogging the screens and preventing the water from flowing into the machine. Clean the filter screens with an old toothbrush, replace them, and try the washer once again. If the water still does not flow properly, install new filter screens; frequently, a thin transparent film of algae can remain in the screens even after cleaning. New filter screens should, however, restore the machine to good working order.

As serious a problem as no water entering your machine may be, it is nothing compared to when the water does not stop and your machine starts to overflow. The

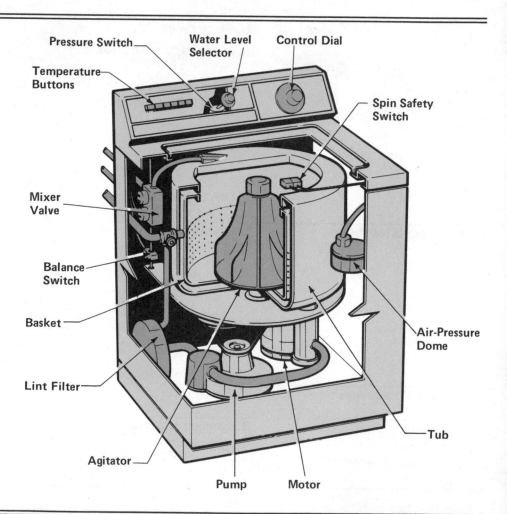

A clothes washer that is not maintained properly can waste a good deal of electricity and hot water. And knowing how to install a new washer can certainly save you money.

first thing to do is to stop the flow of electrical current to the washer; trip the circuit breaker or pull the appropriate fuse. If the water stops, you know the problem lies in an electrical component — either the solenoids on the inlet valves or the machine's water-level switch is malfunctioning and must be replaced.

If the water continues to flow even after you cut off the electricity, turn off the water at the shutoff valves to which the machine's water-inlet hoses are connected. In this situation, the problem is most likely in the water-inlet valve itself. These valves depend on balanced water pressure on both sides of a diaphragm. The balance can be thrown off by sand or rust in the water that somehow gets past the filter screens at the hose terminals. You can disassemble the water-inlet valves to clean them, but a better idea is to prevent valve damage before you are faced with such an emergency situation. Close the machine's shutoff valves whenever you are not washing clothes to relieve the water pressure against the water-inlet valves. Then, at least, you will be facing merely a plumbing problem — not a disastrous flood — if a water-inlet valve should malfunction, a hose leak, and so on.

Installing a Clothes Washer

If you plan to install a new machine, you will need to have both hot and cold water supply pipes handy. If you must extend the water supply pipes to the location of the new washer, simply cut the present pipes, install a T-fitting into each line, and run new supply pipe to the desired location. Then install shutoff valves that have threaded spigots. Such shutoff valves will make your washer installation task much easier because you can then simply attach hoses with threaded couplings to bring the water to the washer. Generally, there are hoses already attached to the washer, and all you have to do is screw the hoses to hot and cold water shutoff valves. A rubber hose washer insures a tight connection.

If you have to install entirely new plumbing when you put in your new clothes washer, be sure to provide shock absorbers or air chambers in the water supply pipelines to prevent water hammer. When you are just attaching hoses to your existing shutoffs, there should be no problem; most likely, the pipes are already equipped with air chambers. But if you have to bring

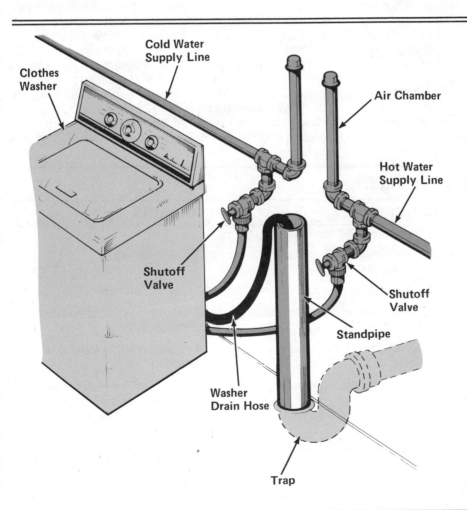

If you have to install entirely new plumbing for a new washer, be sure to provide air chambers or shock absorbers on the water supply pipes. If you do not use a nearby laundry tub for the washer's waste water, you will probably have to install a standpipe drain and trap.

the water supply to the unit via new plumbing, it is essential that you install the air chambers as well. An automatic washer turns the water off and on so abruptly that if there were no air chambers, the water hammer would be unbearable.

As with any fixture, the new clothes washer requires not only supply pipe, but also a means of disposal of the waste. The simplest method is to hook the washer's drain hose over the edge of a nearby laundry tub or sink. If this is not possible, you will probably have to install a standpipe drain and trap. The standpipe should be higher than the highest level that the water reaches in the machine. Check the manufacturer's recommendations. Standpipes, with integral traps, are available in various lengths. To install the standpipe, cut into the house drainage system, install the appropriate waste fitting, and connect the trap and drain.

With the standpipe in place, hook the washer's drain hose onto it. You do not actually attach the hose to the standpipe; just make sure that the end of the hose will stay in place. Push it down into the standpipe about 6 inches, and wedge it in place. Sections from an old automobile tire can work well. Do not seal the hose in place; you want a source of air around the drain hose in the standpipe as a safety precaution. Otherwise, there will be a possibility of a cross-connection between the house's drain system and the plumbing supply lines. Never attach the washer's drain hose directly to any drainpipe.

Here is a hint that has nothing to do with plumbing, but which can give your automatic clothes washer much longer life. When you finally get the unit all hooked up, get out a carpenter's level and make sure that one side of the washer is not higher than the other. Even a small degree of imbalance places an extra strain on the motor.

DISHWASHERS

Dishwashers are, at least insofar as their plumbing is concerned, similar to automatic clothes washers. Most of the plumbing problems you will encounter with a dishwasher will probably have something to do with the water-inlet valves. For example, if water does not enter the dishwasher, the filter screen in the valve may be clogged or else the solenoid that operates the valve is malfunctioning. Similarly, if the water fails to shut off, the valve itself or the solenoid that controls it may be at fault. Very often you can remove the inlet valve or the inlet-valve screen and clean off any residue to solve the problem. Solenoid repair or replacement, however, requires more technical expertise.

Your dishwasher may seem to operate properly, however, and yet your dishes may come out less clean that you think they should be. In such instances, check the instruction manual that came with the unit first to see if it can help you improve the dishwasher's performance. Then, you can check both the water pressure and the water temperature — two extremely important factors in dishwasher operation. The water supply must flow at a rate of at least 2 or 2½ gallons per minute and at a pressure of at least 8 to 10 pounds per square inch. The ideal water temperature is 150°F, but anywhere within the 140°-to-160° range is acceptable. Water that is not at least 140° cannot dissolve grease or detergent. If you run your fingers around your

Clothes Washer Trouble-Shooting Chart

PROBLEMS	CAUSES	REPAIRS
Caution: *Disconnect electrical power to washer before inspecting or repairing.*		
Washer does not fill with water	1. Water shutoff valves on supply pipes closed.	1. Open valves.
	2. Water-inlet hoses kinked.	2. Straighten hoses.
	3. Clogged water-inlet screens.	3. Remove screens and clean out sediment.
	4. Defective water-inlet valve solenoid.	4. Have solenoid repaired or replaced.
	5. Defective water-inlet valve.	5. Disassemble water-inlet valve and inspect for damaged parts. Replace damaged parts or replace entire valve.
	6. Defective timer, water-temperature switch, or water-level pressure switch.	6. Have timer or switch replaced.

Clothes Washer Trouble-Shooting Chart (Continued)

PROBLEMS	CAUSES	REPAIRS
Water does not drain out of washer or washer overflows	1. Kinked drain hose.	1. Straighten hose.
	2. Defective solenoid on water-inlet valve.	2. Have solenoid repaired or replaced.
	3. Clogged water-inlet valve.	3. Disassemble and clean valve.
	4. Defective timer or water-level pressure switch.	4. Have timer or switch replaced.
	5. Slipping or broken drive belt.	5. Tighten or replace belt.
	6. Locked pump.	6. If necessary, have pump replaced.
Agitator does not work	1. Broken drive belt.	1. Replace belt.
	2. Drive belt too loose and slipping.	2. Tighten belt.
	3. Defective transmission.	3. Call service technician.
	4. Defective timer or water-level pressure switch.	4. Have defective switches replaced.
Water drains from machine during wash and rinse cycles instead of at the end of the cycles	1. Drain hose may be lower than water level in basket. Creates vacuum and water siphons out.	1. Reposition drain hose so it is higher than highest water level in washer's basket.
Machine does not spin at all or does not spin at correct speed	1. Broken drive belt.	1. Replace belt.
	2. Slipping drive belt.	2. Tighten belt.
	3. Loose motor drive pulley.	3. Tighten pulley setscrew.
	4. Defective drive clutch.	4. Have clutch replaced.
	5. Spin brake does not release or transmission is frozen.	5. Have one or both repaired.
	6. Defective timer.	6. Have timer replaced.
	7. Open circuit.	7. Call service technician.
	8. Too much detergent.	8. Reduce amount of detergent used.
	9. Clutch needs adjusting (disc type).	9. Have clutch adjusted.
Motor does not operate	1. Power outage.	1. Call power company.
	2. Power cord disconnected.	2. Plug in power cord.
	3. Blown fuse or tripped circuit breaker.	3. Clear circuit. Replace fuse or reset circuit breaker. If same thing occurs, disconnect washer and call service technician.
	4. Defective lid switch.	4. Have switch replaced.
	5. Defective timer.	5. Have timer replaced.
	6. Defective motor.	6. Call service technician.

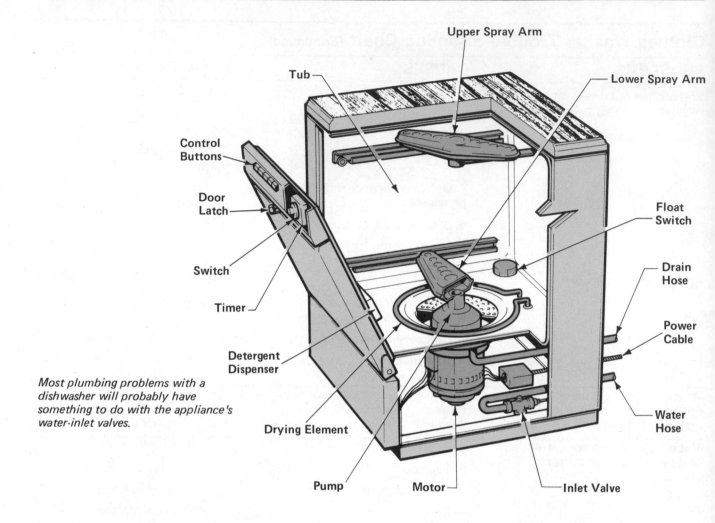

Upper Spray Arm

Tub

Lower Spray Arm

Control Buttons

Door Latch

Float Switch

Switch

Drain Hose

Timer

Power Cable

Detergent Dispenser

Most plumbing problems with a dishwasher will probably have something to do with the appliance's water-inlet valves.

Drying Element

Water Hose

Pump

Motor

Inlet Valve

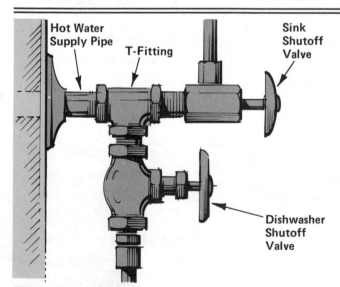

Hot Water Supply Pipe

Sink Shutoff Valve

T-Fitting

Dishwasher Shutoff Valve

The drawing shows how a T-fitting is used to provide a separate shutoff valve for a dishwasher at a sink's hot water supply pipe.

machine and pick up a greasy black film, you know that the water temperature is too low.

Leaks from an automatic dishwasher usually do not occur at the plumbing connections. They are more often the product of door gaskets that have been pulled loose or that are in some other way defective. **Caution:** If you discover a leak in a hose connection, be sure to pull the plug, trip the correct circuit breaker switch, or remove the fuse before you reach under or behind your dishwasher to tighten the loose hose. Were you to touch a live wire while working on a faulty plumbing connection, you would put an early end to your do-it-yourself career.

Installing a Dishwasher

Installing a new dishwasher is easier than putting in some other fixtures because you must hook up only the hot water supply line—cold water is not needed.

While dishwashers may vary in quality and operation, they are pretty uniform in installation procedure. Ideally, the dishwasher should be adjacent to the kitchen sink, on either the right or left side. To install a new dishwasher, follow this general procedure:

Turn off the main water supply and hot water valve at your water heater. Open all house faucets and drain the pipes. Remove the hot water shutoff valve under the kitchen sink and install a T-fitting to the hot water supply stub-out. Reinstall the old shutoff valve that goes to the faucet, and install a new shutoff valve for the dishwasher line directly to the T-fitting. Now run flexible copper tubing from the T-fitting to the inlet valve

on the dishwasher and connect it according to the manufacturer's instructions. Apply plumber's joint compound or tape to all threaded connections.

The drain line from the dishwasher can feed directly into your sink's food waste disposer — attaching to a plug designed for that purpose — or into the sink drainpipe. If you plan to connect the drain line into the sink drain, insert a waste T-fitting in the sink drainpipe between the tailpiece and the trap, or a new tailpiece with a T-fitting for this purpose. If the dishwasher drain hose has a threaded coupling, obtain a waste T-fitting with a threaded connection on its side; otherwise, the drain

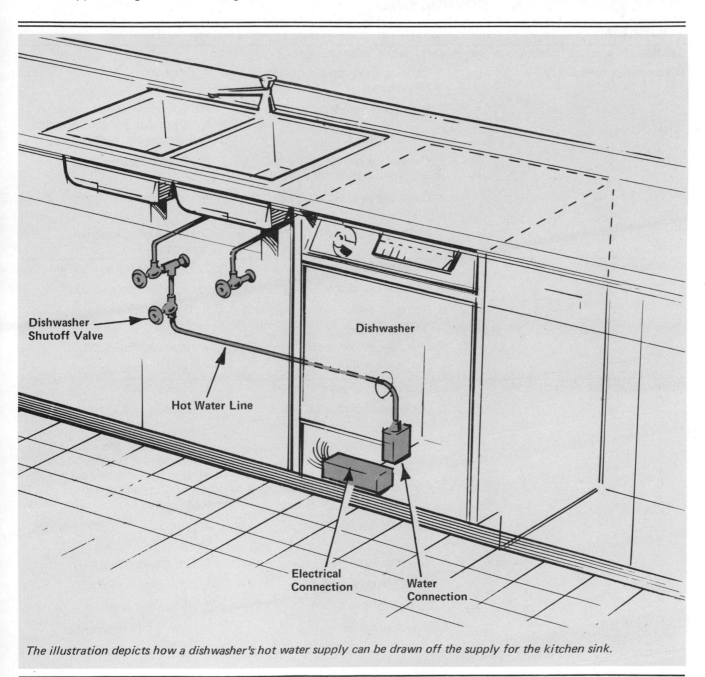

Dishwasher Shutoff Valve

Dishwasher

Hot Water Line

Electrical Connection

Water Connection

The illustration depicts how a dishwasher's hot water supply can be drawn off the supply for the kitchen sink.

hose can be connected to a smooth side connection on the T-fitting by means of a hose clamp.

To connect the dishwasher's drain hose to a food waste disposer that has a short inlet pipe on its side, remove the knockout plug blocking the inlet pipe from inside the disposer. You can angle a screwdriver or punch against the plug and tap the tool with a hammer until the plug comes loose. Remove the plug from the disposer. Connect the drain hose from the dishwasher to the disposer's inlet pipe according to the manufacturer's instructions.

If the dishwasher requires an anti-siphoning device or air gap to operate, connect the dishwasher drain hose to the inlet tube of the anti-siphoning device with a hose clamp. Then connect the device's outlet tube to the food waste disposer with a section of hose and clamps. Or, the device's outlet tube can be connected to a waste T-fitting on the sink drain.

Dishwasher Trouble-Shooting Chart

PROBLEMS	CAUSES	REPAIRS
Caution: *Disconnect electrical power to dishwasher before inspecting or replacing.*		
Dishwasher fails to fill	1. Water shutoff valve is partially or fully closed.	1. Open valve.
	2. Water pressure too low.	2. Pressure must be at least 8 to 10 pounds per square inch. Call local water company.
	3. Clogged water-inlet screen or damaged water-inlet valve.	3. Clean screen or replace assembly.
	4. Defective water-inlet valve solenoid.	4. Have solenoid repaired or replaced.
	5. Faulty float switch, if so equipped.	5. Have switch assembly replaced.
Dishwasher leaks	1. Loose or worn door gasket.	1. Tighten or replace gasket.
	2. Broken door hinge.	2. Have hinge replaced.
	3. Fitting on water-inlet line leaks or line is ruptured.	3. Tighten fitting or replace line.
	4. Defective motor seal.	4. Have seal replaced.
	5. Loose hose clamp.	5. Tighten hose clamp.
Dishwasher does not operate	1. Door not closed and latched.	1. Secure door.
	2. Cycle selection button not fully engaged.	2. Depress button completely.
	3. Blown fuse or tripped circuit breaker.	3. Clear circuit. Replace fuse or reset circuit breaker. If same thing occurs, disconnect power and call service technician.
	4. Overload device tripped.	4. Clear machine; press reset button.
	5. Power outage.	5. Call power company.
	6. Defective door switch.	6. Have switch replaced.
	7. Defective timer.	7. Have timer replaced.
	8. Defective motor.	8. Have motor repaired or replaced.

Dishwasher Trouble-Shooting Chart (Continued)

PROBLEMS	CAUSES	REPAIRS
Dishwasher fails to turn off	1. Defective timer.	1. Have timer replaced.
	2. Water-inlet valve stuck open.	2. Have valve cleaned or replaced.
	3. Clogged water-inlet valve bleed hole.	3. Disassemble valve and clean out bleed hole.
	4. Defective float switch, if so equipped.	4. Have switch assembly replaced.
Dishwasher operates when door is open	1. Faulty door interlock.	1. Have door interlock switch replaced.
Dishes are still wet when cycle is complete	1. Water too cool.	1. Check temperature of hot water supply. Normal temperature is 150°F. Temperature range between 140° and 160° adequate.
	2. Dishware improperly stacked.	2. Restack dishware.
	3. Calcium deposits on heater element.	3. Clean heater element.
	4. Loose connection at heater element.	4. Tighten or repair loose connection.
	5. Heater element burned out.	5. Have heater element replaced.
	6. Inoperative fan motor, if so equipped.	6. Have fan motor replaced.
Dishwasher fails to drain	1. Drain hose kinked or clogged.	1. Remove drain hose, straighten it, and remove any blockage.
	2. Damaged or defective pump.	2. Have pump cleaned, repaired or replaced.
	3. Defective timer.	3. Have timer replaced.
	4. Defective pump motor.	4. Have pump motor replaced.
Dishes come out greasy	1. Insufficient water pressure.	1. Pressure must be at least 8 to 10 pounds per square inch. Call local water company.
	2. Insufficient water temperature.	2. Check temperature of hot water supply. Normal temperature is 150°F. Temperature range between 140° and 160° adequate.

Hot Water Systems

The key to having a trouble-free hot water system is to select a high-quality water heater for your home. Of course, if you already have a water heater, this advice comes too late. Yet, by knowing how to select the proper heater, you may be able to understand some of the problems you may be having with the one that is now in your home. Besides, if your problems become really bad, you may be shopping for a new heater in the near future. Keep these four factors in mind whenever you consider the purchase of a new water heater: size of the tank; warranty on the tank; the tank lining; and recovery time.

People often think that their old water heaters are broken if there never seems to be enough hot water. It may be, however, that the size of the tank is simply not adequate for the size of the family. "It used to do a great job," you say; but stop and think of how your hot water needs have grown. A dishwasher, laundry units, small children — all require plenty of hot water. The tank that was adequate a few years ago may now be overtaxed.

Planning, nevertheless, can expand your present heater's efficiency. Avoid a waiting line at bath time. Change some habits so that the family's baths are spread throughout the day, or some at night and some in the morning. Moreover, quick showers save on hot water. A short shower consumes from 4 to 8 gallons of hot water, while a tub bath can use 20 gallons or more.

Matching Water Heater Size to Family Needs

	Number of People*	Recommended Capacity of Gas Heater (in gallons)				Recommended Capacity of Electric Heater (in gallons)			
		Number of Bathrooms							
		1	1½	2	3	1	1½	2	3
No dishwasher or clothes washer	2	30	30	40	40	30	42	42	42
	3	30	40	40	40	42	42	42	52
	4	40	40	50	50	42	52	52	66
	5	40	50	50	50	52	66	66	82
	6	50	50	50	50**	66	66	66	82
With either clothes washer or dishwasher	2	40	40	50	50	42	42	52	52
	3	40	50	50	50	42	42	52	52
	4	50	50	50	50**	52	52	52	66
	5	50	50	50**	50**	52	66	66	82
	6	50	50	50**	50**	66	66	66	82
With both dishwasher and clothes washer	2	40	50	50	50	42	52	52	66
	3	50	50	50	50	52	52	66	66
	4	50	50	50**	50**	52	52	66	82
	5	50	50	50**	50**	66	66	82	82**
	6	50	50	50**	50**	66	66	82	82**

*Count each child under 10 years of age as two people.
**You might do well to consider having two units.

Arrange to use the automatic dishwasher and the clothes washer at different times of the day, and certainly do not run them at the same time that people are bathing. Avoid running either machine with half loads, and rinse dishes with cold water before you place them in the dishwasher. Many times, we use hot or warm water when cold water could do the job. Modern fabrics are actually designed for cold water washing, and garbage disposers certainly do a much better job with cold water. In addition, you can often use warm water instead of hot water for a great many household chores.

The most popular linings for water heater tanks are glass. Glass linings last much longer than other types, and they generally provide cleaner water. Copper-lined tanks are also good and long-lasting. Galvanized tanks, though way down on the popularity list, can be satisfactory in localities where the water possesses few of the harmful elements that could corrode a galvanized tank. Certainly the least expensive in purchase price, a galvanized tank can prove to be quite expensive if you must replace it after only a couple of years.

In water heater jargon, recovery time usually means the number of gallons per hour that the heater can raise 100°F. Be careful, however; some manufacturers show the recovery rate of their heaters based on a 60° rise. A high recovery rate is very important for families whose schedules force them to consume a great deal of hot water at the same hours of the day.

Another aspect of purchasing a new water heater that you should consider is the method of heating. If you are replacing a unit, it is almost always preferable to stay with the same type of fuel you are currently using. In a new installation, the cost and availability of fuel should be one of your primary considerations. For example, in most cases, a natural gas water heater is less expensive to operate than an electric heater, but an electric one is flameless, can be located in any handy spot (unlike gas) and requires no flue or venting.

If you plan to make the installation a do-it-yourself project, be sure to check with the local building code to see whether there are restrictions as to the type of water heater allowed, and — more importantly — whether you can legally perform the installation yourself. Some communities require that a licensed plumber install a new water heater.

HOW THE WATER HEATER WORKS

The water heater consists of an insulated tank with a source of controlled heat (electric elements or a gas or oil burner), surrounded by a cabinet. If the supply line enters the top of the tank, an internal tube — called a dip tube — carries the cold water to the bottom of the tank. In some heaters, though, the supply line enters the bottom of the tank directly. Since cold water is heavier than hot water, it tends to settle near the bottom. The heated water, in contrast, rises toward the top of the tank. Since the hot water line always exits from the top of the tank, you always get the hottest water available. This construction method also explains why you never run out of hot water gradually. It happens suddenly as the tank empties and the cold water reaches the top of the tank.

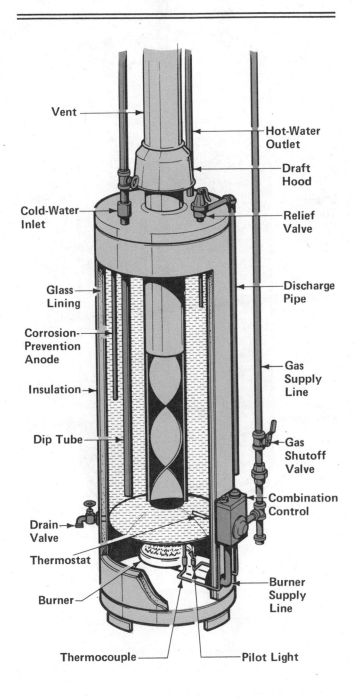

Anatomy of a gas water heater.

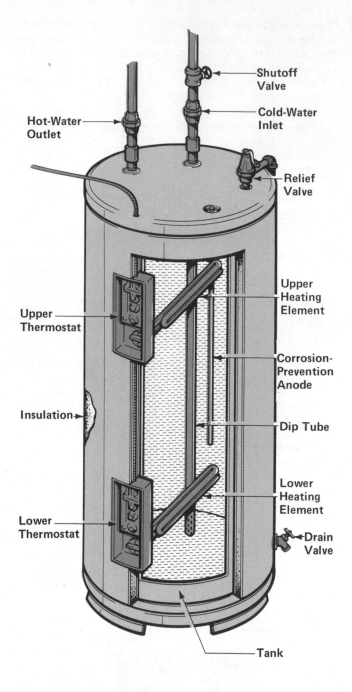

Hot-Water Outlet

Shutoff Valve

Cold-Water Inlet

Relief Valve

Upper Thermostat

Upper Heating Element

Corrosion-Prevention Anode

Insulation

Dip Tube

Lower Thermostat

Lower Heating Element

Drain Valve

Tank

Anatomy of an electric water heater.

Within the tank there is a magnesium rod — called a sacrificial anode — which is placed there to prevent the corrosion of tank parts that may not have been completely treated at the factory. In locations where the water supply is very acidic, the anode itself can be eaten away within a few years. Therefore, the anode is usually accessible through a plug in the top of the tank so that it can be replaced easily.

A bimetal thermostat controls the heat on an electric water heater by turning the heating elements on and off as required to maintain a preset temperature level. The thermostat is adjustable, with a dial scale on the front, although in some instances you have to turn off the power and remove an access panel to reach the dial.

In some cases, the dial indicates temperatures in actual degrees, while other dials just indicate warm, normal or hot (or low, medium or high). Normal (or medium) should be the equivalent of about 140° to 150°F. Always turn the power off before adjusting a thermostat or servicing the heater. Set the thermostat high enough to maintain proper temperatures. Your automatic dishwasher requires hot water of at least 140° to clean your dishes properly, though a temperature setting of around 150° is most desirable. In the absence of a dishwasher, 120° is practical, satisfactory, and economical.

When electricity is the power source, the tank contains heating elements to provide the heat. In most newer heaters, the elements are located within the tank itself. They are bolted onto a flange mounted to the outside of the tank, and a gasket seals the elements against water leakage. Some electric heaters have wrap-around elements; these are metal sheaths that are strapped tightly around the exterior of the tank. Wrap-around elements heat the water throughout the tank.

Most electric heaters have elements and thermostats at top and at bottom. The top element begins to heat first, providing somewhat faster recovery because it is closest to the top of the tank. Since the upper and lower elements are interlocked, the lower element cannot go on until the upper thermostat has turned off the upper element. Then, the lower element turns on, heats the remainder of the tank, and shuts off when the water reaches the correct temperature.

On many electric heaters, a safety interlock is provided. Usually located near the top of the tank and often mounted above the top thermostat, the safety interlock is a device that automatically turns off the power to both elements if the water heater should overheat. To reset it, you must turn off all power to the heater, remove the front access panel, and push a reset button. If the device should kick out a second time, however, be sure to locate and verify the cause. You can use a thermometer at a nearby faucet to determine whether the water is actually overheating.

Gas water heaters also have a thermostat to control the temperature level. The thermostat may be a switch, usually with a tube-type sensing device, that opens and closes a set of electrical contacts; or it may be coupled directly to the gas supply valve itself, using the motion of the expansion and contraction of a temperature-sensitive bellows to open and close the gas valve.

Thermostat controls on some water heaters indicate the temperature range by "low," "medium," and "high" settings. The "medium" setting should be the equivalent of about 140° to 150°F.

With the gas unit, a pilot light is lit at all times, and the flame from the pilot light is directed against a device called a thermocouple. As long as the pilot light is on, the thermocouple sends a message to the gas valve that everything is operating as it should. If the flame goes out, however, the thermocouple cools and sends a message to the gas valve that the pilot light is out. As a result, the gas valve shuts off automatically so that no gas goes to the burner when there is no flame to ignite.

What causes a pilot light to fail? It could be a draft blowing down the vent, or it could be caused by lint collecting near the pilot light's orifice. If your pilot light should fail, look closely around the pilot light area before relighting the flame. If lint has built up, use an old toothbrush to clean it away.

The most common cause for pilot light failure, however, is a faulty thermocouple. Thermocouples are rather inexpensive and easy to replace, but you should be sure to get the proper kind that is the correct length. Thermocouples come with installation instructions. Position the sensing device so that the pilot flame is directed on about the top ½ inch of the thermocouple's tip. It is always a good idea to purchase a spare thermocouple and keep it handy near your heater for emergencies.

Gas water heaters must be vented to the outside of the building. Generally, the flue from the burner passes through the center of the water heater tank to the point where the vent is attached. Baffles within this flue help to divert much of the escaping heat to the interior of the tank where it can be used to heat the water.

In addition to the water heater safety controls already mentioned — the high-limit protector found on most electrical water heaters and the thermocouple on gas water heaters — there is one device that all water heaters should have: a combination temperature-pressure relief valve. The relief valve itself is attached to the top of the water heater tank because that is where the hottest water collects, while the valve's sensing element must be located in the uppermost portion

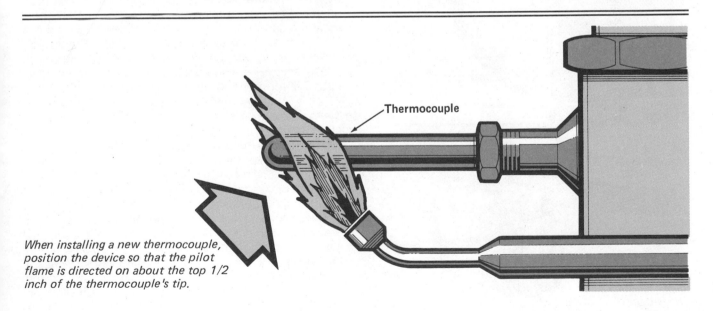

Thermocouple

When installing a new thermocouple, position the device so that the pilot flame is directed on about the top 1/2 inch of the thermocouple's tip.

of the tank. If either the pressure or the temperature within the tank becomes too great, the valve opens releasing steam and excess pressure.

Never underestimate the importance of the water heater's relief valve. With an inoperative valve or with no valve at all, the water heater tank can build up extremely high temperatures and pressure; it can even explode under some conditions, and houses have been leveled by just this one factor. If your water heater does not have a safety valve, turn off the heater and do not turn it on again until you have a relief valve installed. Your heater should also have a discharge pipe connected to the relief valve to carry excess water away from the tank; water expands greatly when heated, and some overflow is not unusual. If the discharge is frequent or copious, have the relief valve and the tank checked; have the valve replaced if necessary.

MAINTENANCE AND REPAIRS

The water heater is one of your home's most important major appliances. It seldom gives any trouble, but when it does, everyone in the household knows about

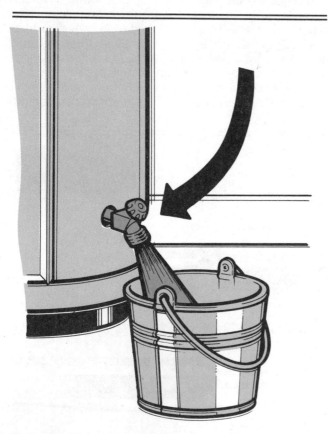

Draining sediment from the water heater tank periodically helps to eliminate noise problems and to keep your heater working more efficiently.

it. Many of the problems that you encounter with a water heater are not generally the kind of repairs for the home handyman, but you will have to decide for yourself whether you can tackle such repairs or whether you should call in professional help. The following information is general in nature, however, and the best guide for trouble-shooting your water heater is the owner's manual you received at the time the unit was purchased.

Caution: Never attempt to make repairs on the burner of a gas water heater. Not only is special equipment required, but there is also a safety factor involved. Only an authorized technician should repair your gas (or oil) burner. Consult your local utility company, and seek their advice when you trace a water heater problem to the burner.

Caution: If you want to make internal repairs on an electric water heater — such as element replacement — be certain that all power to the water heater is turned off before you begin the job. If the water level should fall below the heating elements, the elements would burn out very quickly. Therefore, it is a good idea to turn off the water heater any time you cut the water supply in your home for a long period.

What can you do if you hear strange sounds emanating from the tank? The two most common causes for such noises are steam and sediment in the tank. You can frequently correct steam problems by merely turning the thermostat down (the normal setting is 140° to 150°F), but you may have a faulty thermostat that no longer shuts off the elements or burner when the water reaches the desired temperature. To check the thermostat, turn the setting all the way down. If the heat source does not go out, replace the thermostat. Thermostat failure in an electric heater can result from a short; if it has shorted out, it will have to be replaced.

There is no reason for sediment buildup ever to cause noise — if you check and drain the tank regularly. All you need to do is open the tap of the drain valve (it looks like an outdoor faucet) at the bottom of the tank. Drain off a little water into a container. If it runs clear, stop. If it is not clear, keep draining small amounts until the water does run clear. After a few months, you will be able to determine how often you must follow this procedure. Not only does draining sediment from the tank eliminate noise problems, but it also allows your heater to operate more efficiently.

If your heater is an older model and you have never drained it, your drain valve may have corroded closed. If so, do not force it. It is far better to hold off on draining the tank than to break the valve and flood your home. If your drain valve is stuck, you may have to replace the drain cock — a job that requires shutting off both the heater and the water supply, and then draining the tank before you can remove the faulty valve.

Sediment in the tank may be the reason why you see discolored water coming from your water faucets.

When the anode inside the tank has been attacked by corrosive elements for some time, it can become so corroded that it releases particles that color the hot water you receive at your faucets. If you have this problem, you can usually eliminate it by replacing the anode.

Sediment buildup can also slow down your water heater's recovery rate. If you notice a marked drop in your heater's recovery speed, be sure to drain the sediment from the tank.

When there is no hot water at all, obviously the heat source is out. The first thing to check in a gas unit is whether the pilot light is still on. If it is not, relight it. If the pilot light is still lit, make sure that the valve is turned to "On." Then turn the temperature control knob to its highest position. Turn on a hot water faucet full force, and if the burner does not come on very shortly, your thermostat either needs cleaning or replacement. Usually the control knob slides straight off, and you can take the cover off the thermostat unit by removing a few screws. If you see dirt or corrosion in the thermostat unit, you can usually clean it with a blast of air from a plastic squeeze bottle. If no dirt is present, then you probably have a faulty thermostat that must be replaced.

The first thing to check when an electric heater fails to produce hot water is whether a fuse may be blown or a circuit breaker tripped. If so, clear the electrical circuit. If the heater unit has a short circuit, the fuse will blow again or the circuit breaker will trip again. You must track down the short. Look first at the wiring because the short may only be a loose wire.

If your electric heater has but one element, the problem could be that the element has burned out. With two-element units, however, it is unlikely that both elements would go simultaneously. You can put in a new element yourself, but be sure to cut off both the power supply and the water supply before you start draining the tank. Check the manufacturer's instructions for this job. In some cases, after you remove the element you may discover that it is covered with calcium deposits. If that is what you find, you may be able to clean the element by soaking in vinegar and brushing it before reinstalling it. This procedure is worth trying before buying a new element.

If your utility bills are too high, and you suspect that the water heater is the culprit, check to see whether you have a leak in the plumbing system. Often, a leak can go unnoticed for a long time when it is under the house or inside the walls. Of course, a hot water faucet that leaks can be wasting a great deal of your money every month.

If the tank springs a leak, you may be able to repair it; but you should start shopping around for a new unit. A leak in one spot generally indicates that the tank is corroding, and that a new leak is likely to occur soon after you patch the present one. Patching a water heater tank is usually accomplished with a boiler plug that is inserted into the hole and turned down tight. Sweat-soldering or tightening joints usually can put an end to leaking connections.

Many people complain about the fact that some of their hot water faucets run cold water for what seems like an eternity before any hot water comes out. This situation is not the fault of the water heater. It results from the fact that the heater is so far away from some fixtures that it takes time for all the cold water in the pipes to leave so that the hot water from the tank can come out. If you are really disturbed by having to wait for hot water, then you can have a circulating hot water system installed; such a system keeps hot water at the faucet at all times. The best time to have a circulating hot water system installed, however, is when your house is being built. Another aid in getting hotter water to the faucet faster is to wrap the pipes with special insulating tape; the tape helps stop the pipes from losing heat. The best time to wrap the pipes is, of course, before they are enclosed in the walls.

Water Heater Trouble-Shooting Chart

PROBLEMS	CAUSES	REPAIRS
Caution: *Turn off electrical power or gas supply before servicing heater.*		
Water beneath tank	1. Leaky heating element seal (electric heater).	1. Replace heating element gasket or element.
	2. Leaky plumbing connections.	2. Tighten or replace connections.
	3. Condensation.	3. Not much can be done for this minor problem.
	4. Hole in tank.	4. Hole may be temporarily patched, but tank should be replaced.

Water Heater Trouble-Shooting Chart (Continued)

PROBLEMS	CAUSES	REPAIRS
No hot water	1. Blown fuse or tripped circuit breaker (electric heater).	1. Replace fuse or reset circuit breaker. If same thing occurs, a short circuit exists. Clear circuit, check wire connections or call service technician. DO NOT activate circuit again until it is cleared.
	2. Calcium buildup on heating element(s) (electric heater, immersion type).	2. Remove element(s) and clean.
	3. Upper heating element burned out (electric heater).	3. Replace element.
	4. Defective thermocouple (gas heater).	4. Clean pilot light orifice and relight pilot light. If it refuses to stay lit, replace thermocouple.
	5. Defective thermostat.	5. Replace thermostat.
	6. Safety interlock engaged.	6. Reset safety interlock.
Insufficient hot water	1. Thermostat setting too low.	1. Normal setting is 140° to 150°F; reset thermostat.
	2. Tank too small for requirements.	2. Install larger unit.
	3. Lower heating element burned out (electric heater, immersion type).	3. Replace element.
	4. Defective dip tube.	4. Dip tube may have developed hole, which is allowing cold water to dilute hot water near top of tank. If so, replace it with one recommended by manufacturer.
	5. Low water pressure.	5. Locate and correct problem in water supply or distribution lines.
Slow recovery	1. Calcium buildup on heating element(s).	1. Remove and clean heating element(s).
Steam in hot water	1. Thermostat contacts stuck (electric heater).	1. Examine thermostat for shorted or burned terminals. Replace if required.
	2. Thermostat does not shut burner off (gas heater).	2. If burner fails to go off when thermostat is set lower, replace thermostat.
	3. Thermostat setting too high.	3. Normal setting is 140° to 150°F; reset thermostat.

Private Sewage Systems

People who live in an area where there is no municipal sewage-disposal system must have private sewage systems. The septic tank is now the standard equipment for a private waste-disposal facility, having almost totally replaced the old-fashioned cesspool. The pit privy has also almost disappeared from the scene, but new alternative methods of waste disposal are now appearing, such as the composting-type toilets used in conjunction with separate gray-water disposal systems, and full-cycle waste treatment plants designed for individual residential application.

SEPTIC SYSTEMS

Septic systems often differ in minor construction and operational details, but basically they are similar. Waste travels down the house's main drain to a sewer line and into a large underground tank. Heavier solids settle to the bottom of the tank, forming a layer of sludge. Lighter substances rise to the top, forming a layer of scum. Anaerobic bacteria, enzymes, and fungi go to work on the waste, liquifying most of the solids and reducing the materials to different chemical constituencies. Gases that are formed in the process percolate up through the liquid and the scum layer, and escape through the venting system.

As new waste enters the tank, a like amount of effluent pours from the tank's outlet pipe into a distribution box, from where it is channeled into a network of perforated or loosely jointed drainpipes; it then seeps into the ground and evaporates into the air. During this process aerobic bacteria further reduce the waste until eventually it is rendered harmless. The bacterial action is a natural phenomenon, but the addition of certain chemicals into the system can speed up the liquifying process. What chemicals are used depends on the soil conditions and the type of sewage. Bacterial action can also be quickened by introducing yeast into the septic system. Put about ½ pound of brewer's yeast powder in a bucket of warm water, empty the contents of the bucket into a toilet bowl, and flush it into the septic tank system.

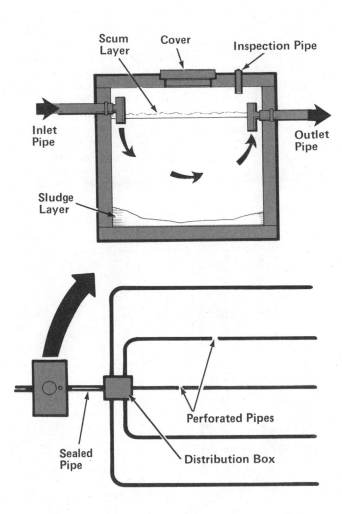

As waste enters the septic tank through the inlet pipe, a like amount exits through the outlet pipe into a distribution box. From there, it flows into a network of perforated or loosely jointed drainpipes and seeps into the ground or evaporates into the air.

TESTING AND CLEANING THE TANK

A septic tank should be checked about once a year, but it may require cleaning only after several years (some tanks go as long as 10 years between cleanings). It is most important that the layers of solids, both top and bottom, never get so close to the opening in the tank's outlet pipe that the solids can be carried out into the drainage field. The same firm that cleans out and removes the solid waste matter can check the tank on an annual basis; but the homeowner can make the inspection himself.

Most tanks have an inspection extension that comes from the top of the tank. Usually a pipe with a screw-on plug, this extension and its plug may be buried only a few inches below ground level. **Caution:** When you uncover and uncap the opening, however, allow the gas in the tank to disperse before you try to make the inspection. Do not breathe the gas; it can asphyxiate you. In addition, make sure that there is no flame or spark around; the gas is explosive.

You have to make a wooden device to test the scum level; fortunately, the scum test stick is easy to make. Hinge a foot-long flap piece of 1x2 to a long 1x2. The hinge allows the flap to fold upward. The exact length of the long piece of 1x2 depends on how deep your tank is buried. Position the flap right at the end of the

long stick, and tie a stout cord to it so that you can fold the hinged flap and hold it next to the stick with the cord. Fold the flap up and insert the stick into the inspection extension vent, forcing it through the layer of scum. After it passes through the layer and beyond the top of the folded-up flap, release the cord. The flap will unfold down. Move the flap until it is against the bottom of the outlet pipe, and make a mark on the stick at the top of the extension pipe. Now, move the flap away from the outlet pipe, bring it up against the bottom of the scum layer; you will feel resistance from encountering the layer of scum. Mark the stick again. The distance between the two marks tells you how close the scum layer is to the bottom of the outlet pipe. If this distance is 3 inches or less, your septic tank needs cleaning.

The sludge test stick is nothing more than a long piece of 1x2 with scrap cloth wrapped and secured around the bottom portion. The length of stick wrapped should equal the distance from the bottom of the outlet pipe opening to the floor of the tank. Place the test stick in the inspection extension pipe, through the scum, and right on down to the bottom of the tank. As the stick goes into the sludge, gently turn it so that the end goes down to the bottom of the tank. The turning also causes the sludge to mark its level on the cloth. Remove the stick slowly. Measure the distance between the top of the sludge layer and the top of the cloth wrap (which is also the bottom of the outlet pipe). Then, consult the sludge allowable table to determine whether the sludge level is high enough to warrant cleaning. The cleaning firm will leave a small layer of the sludge in the tank to assure that the bacterial action will continue uninterrupted.

To inspect your septic tank, you should make two simple testing tools—the scum test stick (left) and the sludge test stick (right).

Table of Allowable Sludge Depth

Tank Capacity (in gallons)	Depth of Liquid (in feet)		
	3	4	5
	Sludge Test Distance from Top of Sludge to Bottom of Outlet Pipe (in inches)		
500	11	16	21
600	8	13	18
750	6	10	13
900	4	7	10
1,000	4	6	8

DISPOSAL FIELDS AND SEEPAGE PITS

The septic tank itself cannot purify the sewage. All it does is liquify some of the solid waste matter. The still-contaminated liquid leaves the tank, and it goes into either a disposal field or seepage pit (the disposal field is usually the better of the two). The liquid goes through the outlet pipe to a distribution box, which is nothing more than a small closed tank with several openings to which pipes are attached to allow the liquid to follow several different routes. From the distribution box, the liquid flows into the disposal or absorption field via pipes that are either perforated or loosely jointed. Released either through the perforations or the loose joints, the liquid waste seeps down into a bed of crushed stone or gravel, and a natural purification process begins.

Where there is not enough room for an adequate drainage field, seepage pits are the answer. Seepage pits, which are really nothing more than large dry wells, can also be utilized where terrain is too steep for easy disposal field construction. The walls of the pits — concrete blocks, bricks or stone — are not generally held together by mortar, so the liquid from the septic tank flows into the pits and seeps through the openings between the blocks, bricks or stones. The bottom of the tank is filled with crushed rock, and sometimes, if the walls weaken, the entire pit fills with loose stones.

CONSTRUCTION AND MAINTENANCE

Generally speaking, the local code, the state health department or some other regulatory body specifies where the septic tank should go, how far it should be from your house, how far from your neighbor's house, how far from your water well (if any), and of what materials the tank and pipe should be constructed. In many areas, two separate septic systems are required. One is for toilet sewage, and the other is for all other waste. There are excellent reasons for having separate systems. For example, the bleaches and detergents used for washing are strong enough to break down or slow the bacterial action necessary for effective operation of the septic tank on toilet sewage. A washing machine itself can put far too much water into a septic tank. The sudden flow of water comes on so strong that it churns up the sludge, and some of the solids that should be dissolved by the bacteria are carried out through the outlet pipe and into the disposal field. The result — clogging — can cause unsanitary conditions.

There are additional substances that can create problems in a septic system. Grease, for example, can be a troublemaker. If there is a place for a grease trap in the kitchen, install one; it can help your septic tank do a better job. It is also bad for your septic tank to have rain water or other surface water drain through the system, and, naturally, foreign compounds should be kept out. If photography is your hobby or if you have some other hobby that requires the use of chemicals, never dispose of such chemicals through your septic tank system.

If you have constant problems with your septic tank system, check with your local authority. You may find that you can alter or enlarge the system to eliminate your troubles.

One of the main considerations at the time of the original septic tank installation should have been the water absorption rate of the soil. If the soil porosity is not right, you may never have a good waste-disposal system. You can test the soil by digging several holes with a post hole digger, going down to the level of the disposal field drainage pipes plus about 6 inches. Fill these holes with water and wait 24 hours. Then, add enough water to the holes until there is about 6 inches of water in each hole. Insert yardsticks in the holes, and time how long it takes for the water level to drop 1 inch. This interval will help you to determine the size of the disposal field you need to do an adequate job. In addition, the width and depth of the trenches under the pipe — as well as the distance between trenches — can also make a significant difference in the efficiency of your septic system.

Soil Porosity and Pipe Chart

Minutes for Water to Drop 1 Inch	Absorption Field Pipe Needed Per Person (in feet)
1	12
2	15
3	17
4	19
5	20
10	30
15	34
20	40
30	60
60	80

The installation of a septic system can be a do-it-yourself project; but the engineering, planning, and layout must follow the standards established in your community's plumbing code. After you have the municipal authority approve your plans, though, most of what remains to be done is plain old manual labor — digging. If you can dig, therefore, you can save plenty of money. This holds true even if you rent digging equipment. The septic tank itself, however, is very heavy; you may want to have professional help to actually place it in position.

A good septic tank system that is properly cared for can be almost problem-free for a long, long time. On the other hand, a poor system or one that is abused can give you trouble every day. If you plan to purchase a home that is equipped with a private sewage-disposal system, it pays to have the old septic tank checked before you buy. The tank could be troublesome or inadequate, and you could be buying a system that will give you more headaches than you ever thought possible.

Glossary

ABS: Acrylonitrile-butadiene-styrene; a plastic used in making pipe.

Adapter: A fitting used to connect pipes, fittings or plumbing fixtures of dissimilar sizes or materials.

Air Chamber: Vertical capped segment of plumbing fixture supply pipe containing air to cushion shock waves created when rushing water is abruptly shut off; a specially made plumbing device made to serve the same purpose.

Air Gap: The distance between a water outlet and the highest possible water level attainable in a plumbing fixture.

Air Vent: See Vent.

Auger: A tool designed to be fed into pipes or fixtures to clean out blockage. Often called a "snake."

Backflow: See Cross-Connection.

Ballcock: An automatic valve device used to control the flow of water into a toilet tank.

Basin Wrench: Tool designed to install or remove locknuts in difficult-to-reach locations.

Branch: Either water or waste offshoots of main pipes that connect to plumbing fixtures.

Branch Vent: A vent pipe running from a vent stack to a branch drain line.

Caulking: Material such as oakum, lead or plastic cement used to seal drainpipe connections, sewer line to septic tank connections, and the like.

Cap: A fitting used to close the end of an open pipe.

Clean-Out: An opening in a drainage pipeline, installed at points of directional change, that allows access for cleaning out blockages.

Clean-Out Plug: A threaded or locking cap used to close and seal a clean-out; also used interchangeably with "clean-out."

Closet: Plumbing term for toilet; also called water closet or stool.

Closet Bend: A 90° fitting used to make a directional change from the closet flange into the horizontal toilet waste pipe.

Closet Flange: A special floor flange for mounting and connecting a toilet to the closet bend and waste line.

Continuous Waste: A waste pipe from more than one fixture, but utilizing a single trap.

Coupling: A fitting used to connect two pipes.

CPVC: Chlorinated polyvinyl chloride; a plastic used in making pipe.

Cross: A four-way fitting used to connect branch sewer lines, used principally in seepage bed grid piping.

Cross-Connection: A dangerous and usually inadvertant open or closed connection between fresh water and drainwater or sewage.

Developed Length: The total measured length of a run of pipe, including pipe and fittings. Measured along the centerline of the pipe.

Disposal Field: The part of a septic tank disposal system that permits absorption into the earth and evaporation into the air of effluent from the tank.

Diverter: A valve that changes the flow of water from one faucet or outlet to another (as between a tub and shower).

Drain: Any pipe that carries away water or waste.

Drain Flange: A flange that attaches to the drain hole in a plumbing fixture and permits the connection of the fixture drainpipe.

Dry Vent: A vent line that carries only air and never water or waste.

DWV: Drain-waste-vent; a term applied to the system of piping and fittings used to carry away drainage and waste and to vent the system; also applied to the pipe and fittings used for that purpose.

Ell: Short for elbow; a fitting used for making directional changes in pipelines; designated in terms of degrees of angle change (e.g. 90° elbow, 45° elbow).

Escutcheon Plate: A plastic or metal plate used to enclose and trim out the rough hole where a pipe stubs through a wall or floor.

Female Thread: The end of a pipe or fitting with internal threads.

Fitting: Any device used to join sections of pipe together, or for connecting pipe to a fixture.

Fixture Drain: A drain line including a trap assembly that extends from the plumbing fixture drain flange to a main or branch waste pipe.

Fixture Unit: A unit of measure describing the amount of waste load a particular fixture discharges; one unit is the equivalent of 1 cubic foot of water per minute.

Flare: Tubing end expanded outward in circular form, creating a pronounced lip of greater diameter than the tubing; a type of fitting designed to seat such a flare on the chamfered end of the fitting body to effect a sealed connection.

Force Cup: A tool used to clear clogs from drains, especially in toilets; also called a "plunger" or a "plumber's helper."

FPT: Female pipe thread.

Frost Line: The depth to which earth freezes in any given area.

FSPS: Female standard pipe size.

Gasket: A device made of compressible material that is inserted and compressed between two mating surfaces to effect a leakproof seal, as in a pipe joint.

Gate Valve: A valve that regulates the flow of water through a gate-like disc within the valve body; flow is either on or off.

Globe Valve: A valve that regulates the flow of water through a spherical, globe-like body; flow is adjustable from on to off.

Grade: The slope of a pipeline.

Group Vent: A vent that functions for more than one trap.

Hanger: A device used to support suspended pipe.

Horizontal Branch: Any offshoot drain running at a slight pitch from a soil or waste stack that collects drainage from fixtures not directly connected to stacks; also called a lateral.

Inspection Panel: A panel allowing access to pipes and traps that are inside a wall or floor; also called an access or service panel.

Joint: Any connection between pipes, fittings or other parts of a plumbing system.

Joint Compound: A compound put on threaded connections to help prevent leaks.

Lateral: See Horizontal Branch.

Lavatory: Plumbing term for washbowl or washbasin; also, a general term for bathroom.

Main: The principal pipe to which branches may be connected.

Main House Drain: The pipe that collects waste from all of the branches going to plumbing fixtures, and delivers it to the main house sewer.

Main House Sewer: The underground pipeline that accepts waste from the main house drain and delivers it to the sewer main or septic system tank.

Makeup: The length of pipe that extends into a fitting socket.

Male Threads: The end of a fitting, pipe or fixture connection with external threads.

MPT: Male pipe threads.

MSPS: Male standard pipe size.

No-Hub: A fitting that couples two lengths of pipe together by means of an external sleeve-and-clamp arrangement.

Offset: A combination of elbows and pipe lengths that moves the pipe run over to a position parallel with the original run.

O-Ring: O-shaped rubber ring used as a seal to prevent leaking.

Packing: Compressible material used to prevent leakage in a joint containing a movable element such as a faucet stem; retained by a packing nut or gland.

PB: Polybutylene; a plastic used in making pipe.

PE: Polyethylene; a plastic used in making pipe.

Pipe Strap: A metal strap used to hang or secure pipe in place on walls, supports or ceilings.

Pipe Support: Any kind of brace used to hold pipes in position.

Pitch: The degree of slope in a run of pipe.

Plunger: See Force Cup.

Pop-Up Valve: A device used to open and close drains.

Potable Water: Water suitable for drinking.

PP: Polypropylene; a plastic used in making pipe.

Putty: A soft sealer material used in certain applications in plumbing systems, and not to be confused with glazier's putty used in replacing window panes; also called plumber's putty.

PVC: Polyvinyl chloride; a plastic used in making pipe.

Reducer: A fitting used to join two pipes of different sizes, usually one trade or nominal size apart.

Riser: A vertical pipe, either main or branch, and usually a supply line.

Rough-In: The complete installation of all plumbing pipes and fittings, but not including plumbing fixtures, trimwork, and most traps; also, the set of dimensions needed to properly lay out pipe stub-out locations to accommodate specific plumbing fixtures during installation.

Sanitary Tee: A fitting with a special curved inside corner used when connecting a horizontal branch to a soil or waste stack.

Septic System: A system of several components used in carrying away, decomposing, and disposing of wastes; employed where connection to a community sewer main is not possible.

Septic Tank: A watertight receptacle that collects waste and converts it through bacterial action to a biodegradable effluent.

Sewer Main: The community sewage line that takes waste from private property to a central sewage plant.

Shutoff Valve: See Stop Valve.

Snake: See Auger.

Soil Pipe: Drainpipe that carries human wastes.

Soil Stack: A vertical pipe that receives human wastes; also, the vertical main pipe that receives both human and nonhuman wastes from a group of plumbing fixtures including a toilet, or from all plumbing fixtures in a given installation.

Spud: The joint connection assembly between a toilet bowl and tank; also called a closet spud.

SR: Styrene-rubber; a material used in making pipe.

Stack: Any vertical main that is a part of the DWV system.

Stop Valve: A manually operated valve in a water supply line used to turn the water off and on; also called a stop or shutoff.

Street Elbow: A fitting used to change pipeline direction, and having a socket at one end but pipe-size at the other end.

Stub-Out: A short length of pipe left protruding from a wall or floor for later fixture connection.

Sump Pump: A special pump used to remove accumulations of water from a sump or shallow pit.

Sweep Elbow: A fitting that makes a long and gentle bend, used in making directional changes in drainpipes.

Tap: A faucet or hydrant for drawing water from a supply line; also, a tool used to cut female or internal threads.

Tee: A T-shaped fitting with three points of connection for pipes.

Trap: A device that permits flow of waste in one direction, but retains a plug of water as a seal or barrier against air and sewer gases in the opposite direction.

Union: A fitting used to join pipes; it allows easy disassembly or disconnection without removing the pipeline.

Valve: A device used to control the flow of water; may be placed in-line (stop) or terminally (faucet).

Vent: A pipe that allows a supply of air into the drainage system to facilitate drainage and prevent backflow of sewer gases through proper siphoning.

Vent Stack: A vertical vent pipe.

Waste-and-Vent Tee: A T-fitting used in drainage systems that provides for the connection of smaller branch drainpipes to a larger main vertical pipe.

Water Closet: See Closet.

Water Hammer: The noise that results when air chambers do not control the force of the rushing water as a faucet is abruptly shut off.

Water Main: The community water supply line that provides water for the house water supply line.

Wet Vent: A pipe that serves for both drainage and venting.

Wye: A Y-shaped fitting used in drainage systems for connecting branch lines to horizontal drainage lines and also to provide clean-outs.